THE AUSTRALIAN
Women's Weekly

Pies

acp
books

CONTENTS

PERENNIAL FAVOURITES

Pies and tarts, both savoury and sweet are among our best-loved foods. They will never go out of fashion – they'll just keep evolving. We love traditional pies: beef pies, spinach and fetta pies from the Middle-East, vegetable pies and quiches, empanadas, shepherd's pie, creamy fish pies. But we also love modern pies that have come about by combining the old traditions with newer flavours: smoked salmon tartlets, thai chicken curry pies, caramelised onion and goat cheese tartlets.

There's a recipe for shortcrust pasty on p 384 with instructions on how to make sweet pastry too. We've also given tips for working with store-bought fillo and puff pastry.

Savoury pies include all the main-course old favourites you'd expect to find – beef pies, lamb pies, fish pies, vegetable pies, chicken pies, but there are also recipes for party pies, pasties, samosas, empanadas and turnovers.

Sweet pies are best if homecooked. Unless you make your own you'll never know the bliss of a great apple pie, rhubarb pie, lemon meringue pie or pumpkin pie.

Savoury tarts & tartlets include well-known quiche recipes but also delicious little tartlets that make great cocktail food, picnic food, lunchboxes and snacks. They're hugely fashionable nowadays, mostly because you can use so many fabulous ingredients in a savoury tart: prosciutto and roasted capsicum; goats cheese and asparagus – but also because they're all quite easy to make and most of them can be eaten hot, warm or cold.

Sweet tarts & tartlets are, like savoury tarts, hard-to-resist treats. From chocolate tarts, cheesecakes and tarte tartin to delicious little Portuguese custard tarts, fruit tartlets, little lemon tarts and fruit mince tarts, there is no better afternoon tea or dessert.

SAVOURY PIES

potato and herb pie

3 medium potatoes (600g)
50g butter
¼ cup (60ml) olive oil
1 medium brown onion (150g),
    sliced thinly
2 tablespoons finely chopped
    fresh flat-leaf parsley
2 teaspoons finely chopped
    fresh thyme
½ cup (125ml) milk

½ cup (125ml) cream
1 egg, beaten lightly
1egg, beaten lightly, extra
1 sheet puff pastry
shortcrust pastry
1 cup (150g) plain flour
90g butter, chilled
1 egg yolk
1 tablespoon lemon juice,
    approximately

1 Make shortcrust pastry.

2 Meanwhile, cut potatoes into 5mm slices. Heat butter and oil in large saucepan; cook potato, in batches, until browned lightly and tender. Drain on absorbent paper; cool. Cook onion in same pan, stirring until onion is soft. Drain on absorbent paper; cool.

3 Roll pastry between baking paper until large enough to line base and sides of a 20cm springform tin. Ease pastry into side of tin; trim edge. Cover; refrigerate 20 minutes.

4 Preheat oven to 200°C/180°C fan-forced. Line pastry case with paper; fill with dried beans or rice. Bake 10 minutes; remove paper and beans. Bake further 10 minutes or until browned; cool.

5 Layer potato, onion and herbs in pastry case; top with combined milk, cream and egg. Brush edge of pastry case with a little extra egg; top pie with puff pastry. Trim edges; gently press edges to seal. Brush pastry with remaining extra egg; prick pastry with fork.

6 Bake pie 15 minutes. Reduce oven to 180°C/160°C fan-forced; bake further 40 minutes or until pastry is browned. Stand pie 10 minutes before serving.

shortcrust pastry Sift flour into large bowl; rub in butter, add egg yolk and enough juice to mix a firm dough. Press ingredients together to form a ball. Cover; refrigerate 30 minutes.

prep + cook time 1 hour 40 minutes (+ refrigeration) **serves** 6
nutritional count per serving 47.6g total fat (24.7g saturated fat);
2692kJ (644 cal); 42.5g carbohydrate; 10.9g protein; 3.1g fibre

crunchy salmon pie

1 cup (150g) plain flour
¼ teaspoon paprika
90g butter, chopped
¾ cup (90g) grated cheddar cheese
filling
3 eggs
300g sour cream
2 tablespoons mayonnaise
few drops Tabasco sauce
210g can red or pink salmon, drained, flaked
½ small onion (40g), grated
1 stalk celery (150g), trimmed, chopped finely
½ cup (60g) grated cheddar cheese

1 Grease a 20cm pie dish (1 litre/4 cups).
2 Process flour, paprika, butter and cheese until crumbly. Reserve ⅔ cup of the flour mixture, then press remaining flour mixture over base and side of dish. Refrigerate until required.
3 Preheat oven to 180°C/160°C fan-forced.
4 Make filling; pour into pastry case. Sprinkle top of pie with reserved flour mixture.
5 Bake pie about 40 minutes or until firm and browned. Serve warm or cold with salad, if desired.
filling Whisk eggs, sour cream, mayonnaise and Tabasco in medium bowl until combined. Stir in salmon, onion, celery and cheese.

prep + cook time 1 hour **serves** 6
nutritional count per serving 47. 9g total fat (28.3g saturated fat); 2500kJ (598 cal); 21.7g carbohydrate; 20.5g protein; 1.4g fibre

lamb and rosemary pies

2 tablespoons olive oil
500g lamb shoulder,
   cut into 2cm cubes
2 medium brown onions (300g),
   chopped coarsely
2 cloves garlic, crushed
1 tablespoon tomato paste
½ cup (125ml) dry red wine
3 small parsnips (360g), chopped

1 tablespoon fresh rosemary leaves
2 cups (500ml) beef stock
fresh rosemary and parsley leaves
1 egg, beaten lightly
pastry
3 cups (450g) plain flour
250g cold butter, chopped coarsely
2 egg yolks
¼ cup (60ml) cold water

1 Heat half the oil in large saucepan; cook lamb until browned all over. Remove from pan.

2 Heat remaining oil in same pan; cook onion and garlic, stirring, until onion is soft. Add paste; cook, stirring, 1 minute. Add wine; bring to the boil. Stir in parsnip, rosemary, stock and lamb; bring to the boil. Reduce heat; simmer, covered, over low heat, 1 hour. Simmer, uncovered, further 45 minutes or until lamb is tender and mixture thickened. Cool.

3 Meanwhile, make pastry.

4 Preheat oven to 200°C/180°C fan-forced. Grease six pie tins (7.5cm base measure, 11cm top). Divide pastry in half; divide one half into six portions. Roll each portion on floured surface until large enough to line tins. Ease six rounds into pie tins; press pastry into sides. Trim edge. Line pastry with foil; fill with dried beans or rice, place tins on oven tray. Bake 15 minutes; remove foil and beans. Bake further 5 minutes or until pastry is lightly browned. Cool 10 minutes.

5 Divide remaining pastry into six portions. Roll each portion on floured surface into small rounds; top with fresh herbs. Gently roll pin over pastry, pressing in herbs and rolling out pastry until large enough to cover pies.

6 Divide lamb mixture among pastry cases, top each with herbed pastry; press pastry top firmly onto base, trim edges. Brush pastry with egg. Bake about 25 minutes or until pastry is golden brown.

pastry Process flour and butter until crumbly. Add egg yolks and enough water to make ingredients just come together. Knead pastry on floured surface until smooth. Cover; refrigerate 30 minutes.

prep + cook time 2 hours (+ refrigeration) **makes** 6
nutritional count per pie 48.8g total fat (26.6g saturated fat); 3490kJ (835 cal); 63.4g carbohydrate; 30.1g protein; 5.2g fibre

snapper and fennel pies

4 medium spring onions (100g), with white bulbs
40g butter
1 large fennel bulb (550g), sliced thinly
2 tablespoons plain flour
1 cup (250ml) fish stock
½ cup (125ml) cream
2 tablespoons finely chopped fennel tops or dill
2 teaspoons dijon mustard
1 tablespoon lemon juice
¼ cup (30g) frozen peas
4 x 200g snapper fillets, chopped coarsely (or any white fish fillet)
2 sheets butter puff pastry
1 egg, beaten lightly

1 Trim spring onions, leaving about 6cm of the stem. Slice thinly.
2 Melt butter in large frying pan; cook onion and fennel, stirring, until onion softens.
3 Add flour to frying pan; cook, stirring, 1 minute. Gradually stir in stock and cream; cook, stirring, until sauce boils and thickens. Stir in fennel tops, mustard, juice and peas. Add fish, stir to combine; remove from heat.
4 Preheat oven to 200°C/180°C fan-forced.
5 Spoon mixture into four 1½-cup (375ml) ovenproof dishes; place on oven tray.
6 Cut four 2cm-wide strips from pastry. Cut four pastry lids large enough to fit the tops of the dishes. Brush dish edges with egg, place pastry strips around edge of dishes; top with pastry lids. Brush with a little more egg.
7 Bake pies about 35 minutes or until pastry is puffed and browned.

prep + cook time 1 hour **makes** 4
nutritional count per pie 46.9g total fat (26.5g saturated fat); 3294kJ (788 cal); 39g carbohydrate; 50.8g protein; 4.2g fibre

spinach and fetta pie

3 x 250g packets frozen spinach, thawed, drained
250g fetta cheese, crumbled
250g ricotta cheese
¼ cup (40g) finely grated parmesan cheese
6 green onions, chopped finely
2 cloves garlic, crushed
2 tablespoons finely chopped fresh dill
1 tablespoon finely chopped fresh mint
1 tablespoon lemon juice
1 egg, beaten lightly
12 sheets fillo pastry
80g butter, melted

1 Preheat oven to 180°C/160°C fan- forced. Grease 24cm springform tin.
2 Squeeze the excess liquid from spinach with hands. Chop spinach finely. Combine spinach in medium bowl with cheeses, onions, garlic, herbs, lemon juice and egg.
3 Layer two sheets of pastry, brushing each with some of the butter. Fold in half lengthways, place in tin, edges overhanging. Repeat with six more sheets, overlapping strips clockwise around pan until covered.
4 Spoon spinach mixture into pastry-lined tin, fold edges back onto filling; brush with butter.
5 Layer remaining four pastry sheets, fold in half crossways; brush with butter. Place on pie, trim pastry a little larger than tin. Tuck pastry edge inside tin.
6 Bake pie about 45 minutes or until browned; cover with foil if it starts to get over-brown. Stand 15 minutes before cutting.

prep + cook time 1 hour **serves** 8
nutritional count per serving 22.5g total fat (13.8g saturated fat); 1438kJ (344 cal); 15.6g carbohydrate; 17.8g protein; 5.4g fibre

veal pie with cheesy semolina topping

1kg diced veal
⅓ cup (50g) plain flour
¼ cup (60ml) olive oil
2 cloves garlic, crushed
2 small brown onions (160g),
    chopped coarsely
2 medium carrots (240g),
    chopped coarsely
2 stalks celery (300g), trimmed,
    chopped coarsely
½ cup (125ml) white wine
400g can diced tomatoes
2 cups (500ml) chicken stock
20g butter, melted
¼ cups (20g) finely grated
    parmesan cheese

gremolata
1 clove garlic, chopped finely
2 tablespoons finely chopped
    fresh flat-leaf parsley
1 tablespoon grated lemon rind
cheesy semolina
3 cups (750ml) milk
1 teaspoon salt
pinch ground nutmeg
⅔ cup (110g) semolina
1 cup (80g) finely grated
    parmesan cheese
1 egg, beaten lightly

1 Toss veal in flour; shake away excess. Heat 2 tablespoons of the oil in large flameproof dish; cook veal, in batches, until browned. Remove veal from pan.
2 Heat remaining oil in same dish; cook garlic, onion, carrots and celery, stirring, until soft. Add wine; boil until almost evaporated. Return veal to pan with undrained tomatoes and stock; bring to the boil. Reduce heat; simmer, covered, 45 minutes. Uncover; simmer 1 hour or until tender.
3 Preheat oven to 200°C/180°C fan-forced.
4 Meanwhile, make gremolata. Make cheesy semolina.
5 Place veal mixture in a 2.5-litre (10-cup) ovenproof dish; sprinkle with half the gremolata. Spoon cheesy semolina over veal, brush with butter; sprinkle with cheese. Bake 25 minutes or until browned lightly. Serve with remaining gremolata.
gremolata Combine ingredients in small bowl.
cheesy semolina Bring milk, salt and nutmeg to the boil in medium saucepan. Reduce heat; gradually stir in semolina, over low heat 5 minutes or until thick. Remove from heat, stir in cheese and egg.

prep + cook time 2 hours 20 minutes **serves** 6
nutritional count per serving 26.7g total fat (11.3g saturated fat); 2546kJ (609 cal); 31.3g carbohydrate; 55.7g protein; 4.1g fibre

easy four-cheese pie

2 sheets butter puff pastry
½ cup (35g) coarse fresh breadcrumbs
1 cup (100g) grated fontina cheese
½ cup (40g) finely grated parmesan cheese
80g blue cheese, crumbled
150g ricotta cheese
⅓ cup finely chopped fresh chives
1 egg, beaten lightly

1 While pastry is semi-frozen, place one sheet of pastry on a board and, leaving a 2cm border, cut slashes with a small, sharp knife 1cm apart.
2 Place a second sheet of puff pastry on a greased oven tray; sprinkle with half the breadcrumbs, leaving a 2cm border. Top with fontina, parmesan and blue cheeses, then small spoonfuls of ricotta. Sprinkle with chives, remaining breadcrumbs and black pepper.
3 Place marked pastry sheet over cheese; press around edges to seal. Freeze 30 minutes or until firm.
4 Meanwhile, preheat oven to 220°C/200°C fan-forced.
5 Brush top of pie lightly with egg; bake about 20 minutes or until golden brown. Serve with a crisp green salad, if you like.

prep + cook time 40 minutes (+ freezing) **serves** 4
nutritional count per serving 28.3g total fat (16.4g saturated fat); 1768kJ (423 cal); 24.3g carbohydrate; 17.5g protein; 1g fibre

beef and red wine pies

1kg chuck steak, diced
⅓ cup (50g) plain flour
2 tablespoons olive oil
1 large brown onion (200g),
  chopped finely
1 clove garlic, crushed
1 large carrot (180g), chopped
1 stalk celery (150g), trimmed,
  chopped
1 tablespoon tomato paste
2 bay leaves

1 cup (250ml) red wine
1½ cups (375ml) beef stock
2 tablespoons coarsely chopped
  flat-leaf parsley
pastry
1½ cups (225g) plain flour
125g cold butter, chopped
1 egg yolk
1 tablespoon iced water,
  approximately
1 egg, beaten lightly

1 Toss steak in flour, shake away excess. Heat oil in large saucepan; cook steak, in batches, until browned. Remove from pan. Add onion, garlic, carrot and celery to same pan; cook, stirring, until softened. Add tomato paste and bay leaves; cook further 2 minutes. Add wine; bring to the boil. Return steak to pan with stock; simmer, covered, over low heat, 1½ hours. Remove lid, simmer, uncovered, a further 30 minutes or until tender, stirring occasionally. Stir in parsley.

2 Meanwhile, make pastry.

3 Preheat oven to 200°C/180°C fan-forced. Grease six 1¼-cup (300ml) pie dishes; place dishes on oven tray. Divide beef mixture among dishes.

4 Divide pastry into six portions. Roll out each portion on floured surface until slightly larger than tops of dishes. Cut thin strips from edge of each pastry portion to line top edge of pie dishes. Place remaining pastry rounds on top of dishes; trim edges. Crimp edge of the pastry. Brush top of pies with egg.

5 Bake pies about 25 minutes or until pastry is browned and filling hot.

pastry Process flour and butter until crumbly. Add egg yolk and enough of the water until mixture just comes together. Knead pastry gently on floured surface until smooth. Cover; refrigerate 30 minutes.

prep + cook time 2 hours 30 minutes **makes** 6
nutritional count per pie 38.2g total fat (17.6g saturated fat); 2964kJ (709 cal); 37.6g carbohydrate; 45.6g protein; 3.5g fibre

vegetable pithiviers with tomato sauce

10 large egg tomatoes (900g),
  quartered
2 teaspoons brown sugar
⅓ cup (80ml) olive oil
2 tablespoons red wine vinegar
2 large red capsicums (700g)
30g butter
2 large green zucchini (300g),
  sliced thinly

7 flat mushrooms (560g),
  sliced thinly
1 clove garlic, crushed
1 tablespoon port
5 sheets puff pastry, thawed
1 egg yolk
1 tablespoon milk
50g baby spinach leaves

1 Preheat oven to 180°C/160°C fan-forced. Grease oven trays.
2 Combine tomato, sugar, half of the oil and half of the vinegar in large bowl; place tomato pieces, skin-side down, on oven tray. Roast 1 hour 40 minutes. Remove from oven; return to same bowl; crush with potato masher. Cover to keep warm; reserve tomato sauce.
3 Halve capsicums, place pieces skin-side up, on oven tray. Roast in oven 40 minutes or until softened. Place capsicum in plastic bag; close tightly, cool. Discard skin, membrane and seeds; slice thinly.
4 Meanwhile, melt butter in large frying pan; cook zucchini, stirring, about 5 minutes or until softened. Place zucchini in small bowl; cover to keep warm. Cook mushrooms and garlic in same pan, stirring, about 5 minutes or until mushrooms soften. Add port; cook, stirring, until liquid evaporates.
5 Cut four of the pastry sheets into 16cm squares; cut remaining sheet into quarters. Place one of the small squares on oven tray; centre 9cm cutter on pastry. Layer a quarter of the mushroom mixture, a quarter of the zucchini and a quarter of the capsicum on pastry; remove cutter. Brush border with combined egg yolk and milk; top with one of the large squares, press edges together to seal.
6 Using sharp knife, cut around pithiviers, leaving 5mm border; mark pastry with swirl design from centre to side, without cutting through. Brush with egg mixture. Repeat with remaining pastry, vegetables and egg mixture. Bake about 25 minutes.
7 Combine spinach, remaining oil and remaining vinegar in small bowl. Serve pithivier with tomato sauce and salad.

prep + cook time 2 hours 30 minutes **makes** 4
nutritional count per pithivier 74.3g total fat (10.5g saturated fat); 4824kJ (1154 cal); 90.9g carbohydrate; 23.5g protein; 12.3g fibre

chicken and olive empanadas

2 cups (500ml) chicken stock
1 bay leaf
3 chicken thigh fillets (330g)
1 tablespoon olive oil
1 small brown onion (80g), chopped finely
2 cloves garlic, crushed
2 teaspoons ground cumin
½ cup (80g) sultanas
⅓ cup (40g) coarsely chopped seeded green olives
5 sheets shortcrust pastry, thawed
1 egg, beaten lightly

1 Place stock and bay leaf in medium frying pan; bring to the boil. Add chicken, reduce heat; poach chicken, covered, about 10 minutes or until cooked through. Cool chicken in liquid 10 minutes; shred chicken finely. Reserve 1 cup of the poaching liquid; discard remainder.
2 Meanwhile, heat oil in large frying pan; cook onion, stirring, until softened. Add garlic and cumin; cook, stirring, until fragrant. Add sultanas and reserved poaching liquid; bring to the boil. Reduce heat; simmer, uncovered, about 15 minutes or until liquid is almost evaporated. Stir in chicken and olives.
3 Preheat oven to 200°C/180°C fan-forced. Grease two oven trays.
4 Using 9cm cutter, cut 24 rounds from pastry sheets. Place 1 level tablespoon of the filling in centre of each round; fold round in half to enclose filling, pinching edges to seal. Using fork, press around edges of empanadas. Place on trays; brush tops with egg.
5 Bake empanadas about 25 minutes. Serve with yogurt.

prep + cook time 45 minutes **makes** 24
nutritional count per empanada 12g total fat (5.6g saturated fat); 849kJ (203 cal); 18.3g carbohydrate; 5.5g protein; 0.9g fibre

pumpkin and fetta pies

500g pumpkin, cut into 2cm pieces
3 eggs
200g fetta cheese, cut into 2cm pieces
2 tablespoons finely grated parmesan cheese
2 tablespoons sour cream
⅓ cup (80g) drained char-grilled capsicum in oil, sliced thinly
2 tablespoons halved seeded black olives
4 green onions, sliced thinly
1 sheet puff pastry, thawed
1 teaspoon finely shredded fresh basil

1 Preheat oven to 220°C/200°C fan-forced. Grease four 11cm pie tins.
2 Boil, steam or microwave pumpkin until tender; drain.
3 Meanwhile, combine eggs, cheeses, sour cream, capsicum, olives and green onion in large bowl. Add pumpkin; mix gently.
4 Cut pastry sheet into four squares; press each square into a tin, allowing pastry to hang over edge. Place tins on oven tray; divide filling among tins.
5 Bake pies about 15 minutes or until filling sets. Sprinkle with basil before serving.

prep + cook time 30 minutes **makes** 4
nutritional count per pie 31.7g total fat (13.5g saturated fat); 1956kJ (468 cal); 24.3g carbohydrate; 21g protein; 2.1g fibre

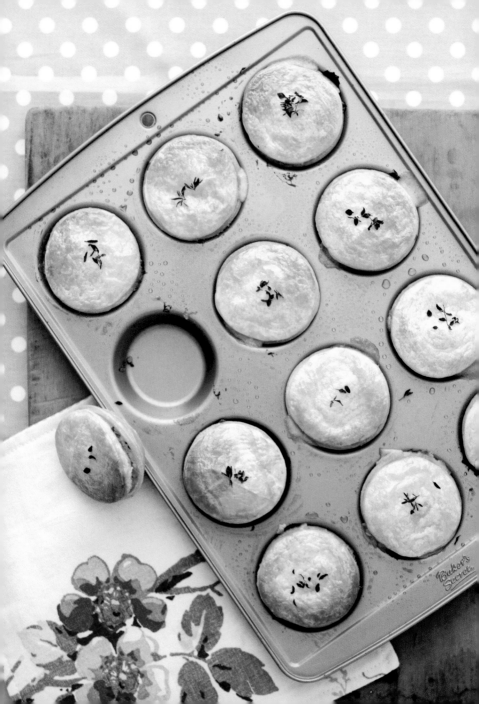

little chicken and leek pies

¾ cup (180ml) chicken stock
½ cup (125ml) dry white wine
2 single chicken breast fillets (340g)
20g butter
1 medium leek (350g), chopped finely
1 stalk celery (150g), trimmed, chopped finely
1 tablespoon plain flour
2 teaspoons fresh lemon thyme leaves
½ cup (125ml) cream
1 teaspoon dijon mustard
4 sheets shortcrust pastry
3 sheets puff pastry
1 egg yolk, beaten lightly
lemon thyme leaves, extra

1 Bring stock and wine to the boil in medium saucepan. Add chicken; return to the boil. Cover; reduce heat, simmer about 10 minutes or until chicken is just cooked through. Remove from heat; stand chicken 10 minutes. Remove chicken, reserve ¾ cup (180ml) cooking liquid; chop chicken finely.
2 Melt butter in medium saucepan; cook leek and celery, stirring, until soft. Add flour and thyme, stir until bubbling. Gradually stir in reserved cooking liquid and cream; cook, stirring, until mixture boils and thickens. Stir in chicken and mustard. Remove from heat, cool slightly.
3 Preheat oven to 220°C/200°C fan-forced. Grease three 12-hole patty pans.
4 Using 7cm cutter, cut 36 rounds from shortcrust pastry. Press into pan holes. Spoon 1 tablespoon of chicken mixture into each pastry case.
5 Using 6cm cutter, cut 36 rounds from puff pastry. Top chicken mixture with pastry lids, brush with egg yolk and sprinkle with extra thyme.
6 Bake pies about 15 minutes or until browned.

prep + cook time 1 hour (+ cooling) **makes** 36
nutritional count per pie 10.5g total fat (4.3g saturated fat); 715kJ (171 cal); 13.9g carbohydrate; 4.4g protein; 0.8g fibre

beef, tomato and pea pies

1 tablespoon vegetable oil
1 small brown onion (80g), chopped finely
300g beef mince
400g can crushed tomatoes
1 tablespoon tomato paste
2 tablespoons worcestershire sauce
½ cup (125ml) beef stock
½ cup (60g) frozen peas
3 sheets puff pastry
1 egg, beaten lightly

1 Heat oil in large saucepan; add onion, cook, stirring, until softened. Add beef; cook, stirring, until changed in colour. Stir in undrained crushed tomatoes, paste, sauce and stock; bring to the boil. Reduce heat, simmer, uncovered, about 20 minutes or until sauce thickens. Stir in peas. Cool.
2 Preheat oven to 200°C/180°C fan-forced. Oil six-hole (¾-cup/180ml) texas muffin pan.
3 Cut two 13cm rounds from opposite corners of each pastry sheet; cut two 9cm rounds from remaining corners of each sheet. Place large pastry rounds in pan holes to cover bases and sides; trim any excess pastry. Lightly prick bases with a fork; refrigerate 30 minutes.
4 Line each pastry-lined pan hole with baking paper; fill holes with dried beans or rice. Bake 10 minutes; remove paper and beans. Cool.
5 Spoon beef mixture into pastry cases; brush edges with a little egg. Top pies with small pastry rounds, pressing edges to seal. Brush pies with remaining egg.
6 Bake pies about 15 minutes or until browned lightly. Stand 5 minutes in pan before serving. Serve with mashed potato, if you like.

prep + cook time 1 hour (+ standing & refrigeration) **makes** 6
nutritional count per pie 26.7g total fat (3.5g saturated fat); 1914kJ (458 cal); 35.4g carbohydrate; 17.9g protein; 3g fibre

lamb korma pies

20g butter
2 tablespoons olive oil
600g lamb fillets,
  chopped coarsely
1 medium brown onion (150g),
  sliced thinly
1 clove garlic, crushed
2cm piece fresh ginger (10g),
  grated
¼ cup (20g) roasted flaked
  almonds

⅓ cup (100g) korma paste
⅓ cup (80ml) chicken stock
½ cup (140g) yogurt
1 cup (120g) frozen peas
1 tablespoon lemon juice
⅓ cup firmly packed fresh
  coriander leaves
6 sheets puff pastry
1 egg, beaten lightly

1 Heat half the butter with half the oil in large saucepan; cook lamb, in batches, until browned. Remove from pan.
2 Heat remaining butter and oil in same pan; cook onion, garlic and ginger, stirring, until onion softens. Add nuts and paste; cook, stirring, until fragrant.
3 Return lamb to pan with stock and yogurt; simmer, uncovered, about 20 minutes or until sauce thickens. Stir in peas, juice and coriander. Cool.
4 Oil two six-hole (¾-cup/180ml) texas muffin pans. Cut two 13cm rounds from opposite corners of each pastry sheet; cut two 9cm rounds from remaining corners of each sheet. Place large pastry rounds in pan holes to cover bases and sides; trim any excess pastry. Lightly prick bases with fork; refrigerate 30 minutes. Cover small pastry rounds with damp cloth; refrigerate.
5 Preheat oven to 200°C/180°C fan-forced.
6 Line each pastry-lined pan hole with baking paper; fill with dried beans or rice. Bake 10 minutes; remove paper and beans. Cool.
7 Spoon lamb mixture into pastry cases; brush pastry edges with egg. Top pies with small pastry rounds, pressing edges to seal. Brush pies with remaining egg.
8 Bake pies about 15 minutes. Stand 5 minutes in pan before serving. Serve with mango chutney and raita, if you like.

prep + cook time 1 hour 15 minutes (+ refrigeration) **makes** 12
nutritional count per pie 29.6g total fat (13.1g saturated fat);
1977kJ (473 cal); 32.9g carbohydrate; 17.7g protein; 3g fibre

chicken, mushroom and fennel pies

1 tablespoon olive oil
2 cloves garlic, crushed
1 medium leek (350g), sliced thinly
1 small fennel bulb (200g), sliced thinly
200g button mushrooms, quartered
½ cup (125ml) dry white wine
4 breast fillets (800g), chopped coarsely
300ml cream
1 tablespoon dijon mustard
¼ cup coarsely chopped fresh flat-leaf parsley
1 sheet puff pastry, cut into quarters
1 egg, beaten lightly
1 tablespoon fennel seeds

1 Preheat oven to 200°C/180°C fan-forced.
2 Heat oil in large saucepan; cook garlic, leek, fennel and mushrooms, stirring, until vegetables soften.
3 Stir in wine; bring to the boil. Reduce heat; simmer, uncovered, 3 minutes. Add chicken and cream; bring to the boil. Reduce heat; simmer, uncovered, about 10 minutes or until chicken is cooked through and sauce thickened slightly. Stir in mustard and parsley.
4 Meanwhile, place pastry quarters onto oven tray, brush pastry with egg then sprinkle with seeds; bake about 10 minutes or until golden brown.
5 Divide chicken mixture among small serving bowls, top each with pastry; serve with rocket salad, if you like.

prep + cook time 40 minutes **serves** 4
nutritional count per serving 52.8g total fat (28.8g saturated fat); 3340kJ (799 cal); 20.9g carbohydrate; 54g protein; 4.4g fibre

shepherd's pie

30g butter
1 medium brown onion (150g), chopped finely
1 medium carrot (120g), chopped finely
½ teaspoon dried mixed herbs
4 cups (750g) finely chopped cooked lamb
¼ cup (70g) tomato paste
¼ cup (60ml) tomato sauce
2 tablespoons worcestershire sauce
2 cups (500ml) beef stock
2 tablespoons plain flour
⅓ cup (80ml) water
potato topping
5 medium potatoes (1kg), chopped coarsely
60g butter
¼ cup (60ml) milk

1 Preheat oven to 200°C/180°C fan-forced. Oil shallow 2.5 litre (10 cup) ovenproof dish.
2 Make potato topping.
3 Meanwhile, heat butter in large saucepan; cook onion and carrot, stirring, until tender. Add mixed herbs and lamb; cook, stirring, 2 minutes. Stir in paste, sauces and stock, then blended flour and the water; stir over heat until mixture boils and thickens. Pour mixture into dish. Drop heaped tablespoons of potato topping onto lamb mixture.
4 Bake pie about 20 minutes or until browned and heated through.
potato topping Boil, steam or microwave potato until tender; drain. Mash with butter and milk until smooth.

prep + cook time 1 hour **serves** 4
nutritional count per serving 36.2g total fat (20.2g saturated fat); 2976kJ (712 cal); 44.7g carbohydrate; 48.8g protein; 6g fibre

meat pies

1½ cups (225g) plain flour
100g cold butter,
  chopped coarsely
1 egg
1 tablespoon iced water,
  approximately
2 sheets puff pastry
1 egg, extra

beef filling
1 tablespoon vegetable oil
1 small brown onion (80g),
  chopped finely
600g beef mince
415g can crushed tomatoes
2 tablespoons tomato paste
2 tablespoons worcestershire
  sauce
¾ cup (180ml) beef stock

1 Process flour and butter until crumbly. Add egg and enough of the water to make ingredients cling together. Knead pastry on floured surface until smooth. Cover; refrigerate 30 minutes.

2 Meanwhile, make beef filling.

3 Oil six ⅔ cup (160ml) pie tins. Divide pastry into six portions; roll each portion between sheets of baking paper until large enough to line tins. Lift pastry into tins; gently press over base and sides. Trim edges. Refrigerate 30 minutes.

4 Cut six 11cm rounds from puff pastry. Refrigerate until required.

5 Preheat oven to 200°C/180°C fan-forced.

6 Line pastry-lined tins with baking paper; fill with dried beans or rice. Place tins on oven tray; bake 10 minutes. Remove paper and beans; bake further 5 minutes. Cool.

7 Fill pastry cases with beef filling; brush edges of pastry with extra egg. Top with puff pastry rounds; press edges to seal. Brush tops with egg. Cut steam holes in top of pies.

8 Bake pies about 20 minutes or until pastry is golden.

beef filling Heat oil in large saucepan; cook onion and mince, stirring, until mince is well browned. Stir in undrained tomatoes, paste, sauce and stock; bring to the boil. Reduce heat; simmer, uncovered, about 20 minutes or until thick. Cool.

prep + cook time 1 hour 35 minutes (+ refrigeration) **makes** 6
nutritional count per pie 38.7g total fat (13.8g saturated fat); 2876kJ (688 cal); 52.4g carbohydrate; 31.2g protein; 3.5g fibre

chicken and leek pie

2 cups (500ml) chicken stock
600g chicken breast fillets
1 tablespoon olive oil
40g butter
1 large leek (500g), sliced thinly
2 stalks celery (300g), trimmed, chopped finely
2 tablespoons plain flour
2 teaspoons fresh thyme leaves
½ cup (125ml) milk
1 cup (250ml) cream
2 teaspoons wholegrain mustard
2 sheets shortcrust pastry
1 sheet puff pastry
1 egg yolk

1 Bring stock to the boil in medium saucepan. Add chicken; return to the boil. Reduce heat; simmer, covered, about 10 minutes or until chicken is cooked. Remove from heat; stand chicken in poaching liquid 10 minutes. Remove chicken; chop coarsely. Reserve ⅓ cup of the poaching liquid; keep remainder for another use, or discard.
2 Heat oil and butter in medium saucepan; cook leek and celery, stirring, until leek softens. Add flour and thyme; cook, stirring, 1 minute. Gradually stir in reserved poaching liquid, milk and cream; cook, stirring, until mixture boils and thickens. Stir in chicken and mustard. Cool 10 minutes.
3 Preheat oven to 200°C/180°C fan-forced. Oil 1.5 litre (6 cup) ovenproof dish.
4 Line base and side of dish with shortcrust pastry, trim to fit; prick well all over with fork. Bake 10 minutes. Cool 5 minutes.
5 Spoon chicken mixture into pastry case; place puff pastry over filling, trim to fit dish. Brush pastry with egg yolk; cut two small slits in top of pastry. Bake about 20 minutes or until browned lightly.

prep + cook time 1 hour 35 minutes **serves** 6
nutritional count per serving 56g total fat (30.1g saturated fat); 3344kJ (800 cal); 42.5g carbohydrate; 31.1g protein; 3.6g fibre

beef bourguignon pies

12 pickling onions (480g)
6 bacon rashers (420g),
   rind removed, sliced thinly
2 tablespoons olive oil
400g mushrooms
1kg gravy beef, trimmed,
   cut into 2cm pieces
¼ cup (35g) plain flour
1 tablespoon tomato paste

2 teaspoons fresh thyme leaves
1 cup (250ml) dry red wine
2 cups (500ml) beef stock
2 sheets butter puff pastry
cooking-oil spray
½ cup finely chopped fresh
   flat-leaf parsley

1 Peel onions, leaving roots intact; halve lengthways.

2 Cook bacon in heated large saucepan, stirring, until crisp; drain on absorbent paper. Reheat same pan; cook onion, stirring, until browned all over, remove from pan. Heat 2 teaspoons of the oil in same pan; cook mushrooms, stirring, until just browned, remove from pan.

3 Coat beef in flour; shake off excess. Heat remaining oil in same pan; cook beef, in batches, until browned all over. Return beef and any juices to pan, add bacon and onion with tomato paste and thyme; cook, stirring, 2 minutes. Add wine and stock; bring to the boil. Reduce heat; simmer, covered, 1 hour. Add mushrooms; simmer, uncovered, about 40 minutes or until beef is tender, stirring occasionally.

4 Meanwhile, preheat oven to 220°C/200°C fan-forced.

5 Place pastry sheets on board; using 1¼ cup (310ml) ovenproof dish as a guide, cut out six pastry rounds using the tip of a knife. Place pastry rounds on oiled oven tray, spray with cooking-oil spray; bake about 5 minutes or until lids are browned lightly.

6 Meanwhile, stir parsley into beef bourguignon then divide among dishes. Top each pie with pastry lid. Serve pies with hot chips, if you like.

prep + cook time 2 hours **makes** 6
nutritional count per pie 36.4g total fat (8.5g saturated fat); 2817kJ (674 cal); 23.5g carbohydrate; 55g protein; 3.4g fibre

tuna and fetta turnovers

425g can tuna in oil
100g ricotta cheese
100g fetta cheese, crumbled
50g sun-dried tomatoes, sliced thinly
2 teaspoons drained baby capers
2 tablespoons finely chopped fresh flat-leaf parsley
2 tablespoons roasted pine nuts
1 tablespoon lemon juice
4 sheets puff pastry, thawed
2 tablespoons milk

1 Drain tuna over a bowl; reserve 2 tablespoons of the tuna oil. Flake tuna into medium bowl, add cheeses, tomato, capers, parsley, nuts, juice and reserved tuna oil; mix well.
2 Preheat oven to 200°C/180°C fan-forced. Grease oven trays.
3 Cut four 12cm rounds from each pastry sheet. Place one heaped tablespoon of tuna mixture on each round; brush edges with a little milk, fold over to enclose filling. Press edges to seal; repeat with remaining tuna mixture and pastry. Place on trays; brush lightly with milk.
4 Bake turnovers about 15 minutes or until browned lightly.

prep + cook time 35 minutes **makes** 16
nutritional count per serving 18.5g total fat (3g saturated fat); 1141kJ (273 cal); 16.4g carbohydrate; 10g protein; 1.1g fibre

creamy fish pie

10g butter
2 teaspoons olive oil
1 small brown onion (80g), chopped finely
1 medium carrot (120g), chopped finely
1 stalk celery (150g), trimmed, chopped finely
1 tablespoon plain flour
1 cup (250ml) fish stock
500g firm white fish fillets, chopped coarsely
½ cup (125ml) cream
1 tablespoon english mustard
1 cup (120g) frozen peas
½ cup (40g) finely grated parmesan cheese
1 sheet puff pastry
1 egg, beaten lightly

1 Preheat oven to 220°C/200°C fan-forced.
2 Melt butter with oil in large saucepan; cook onion, carrot and celery, stirring, until carrot softens. Stir in flour; cook, stirring, 2 minutes. Add stock and fish; cook, stirring, until fish is cooked through and mixture boils and thickens. Remove from heat; stir in cream, mustard, peas and cheese.
3 Spoon mixture into a shallow small 1.5-litre (6-cup) baking dish; top with pastry. Brush top with egg.
4 Bake pie about 20 minutes or until browned.

prep + cook time 40 minutes **serves** 4
nutritional count per serving 35.1g total fat (19.1g saturated fat); 2366kJ (566 cal); 23.5g carbohydrate; 37.5g protein; 4.1g fibre
tips It is important you use a shallow baking dish so that the top of the fish mixture is touching the pastry and the pastry is not stuck to the sides of the dish, as this could prevent it from rising.
You can use any firm white fish fillet you like in this recipe, for example, blue-eye, ling or snapper.

liver, mushroom and bacon pies

500g lamb liver
2 tablespoons olive oil
1 clove garlic, crushed
1 medium brown onion (150g), chopped finely
4 rindless bacon rashers (260g), chopped coarsely
200g button mushrooms, quartered
2 tablespoons plain flour
½ cup (125ml) dry red wine
1½ cups (375ml) beef stock
1kg packet frozen shoestring chips
1 sheet butter puff pastry
1 egg yolk
1 tablespoon milk

1 Preheat oven to 220°C/200°C fan-forced. Line oven tray with baking paper.
2 Discard membrane and any fat from liver; chop coarsely. Heat half of the oil in large frying pan; cook liver, in batches, over high heat until browned and cooked as desired.
3 Heat remaining oil in same pan; cook garlic, onion, bacon and mushrooms, stirring, until onion softens. Add flour; cook, stirring, until mixture thickens and bubbles. Gradually add wine and stock; stir until mixture boils and thickens. Return liver to pan.
4 Meanwhile, cook chips, in oven, according to packet instructions.
5 Cut four 9.5cm rounds from pastry sheet; place on tray, brush with combined egg and milk. Bake, uncovered, with chips about 5 minutes or until rounds are browned lightly.
6 Divide liver mixture among four 1¼-cup (310ml) ramekins; top with pastry rounds, serve with chips.

prep + cook time 35 minutes **serves** 4
nutritional count per serving 60.2g total fat (13.4g saturated fat); 5543kJ (1326 cal); 136.9g carbohydrate; 53.3g protein; 14.1g fibre

lamb and pea pies

2 tablespoons olive oil
400g diced lamb
4 baby onions (100g), quartered
1 tablespoon plain flour
¼ cup (60ml) dry red wine
¾ cup (180ml) beef stock
1 tablespoon tomato paste
1 tablespoon fresh rosemary
  leaves

2 sheets puff pastry
1 egg, beaten lightly
4 fresh rosemary sprigs
20g butter
2½ cups (300g) frozen peas
1 tablespoon lemon juice
½ cup (125ml) water

1 Heat half of the oil in large saucepan; cook lamb, in batches, uncovered, until browned all over. Remove from pan.

2 Heat remaining oil in same pan; cook onion, stirring, until soft. Add flour; cook, stirring, until mixture bubbles and thickens. Gradually add wine, stock, paste and rosemary leaves; stir until mixture boils and thickens. Stir in lamb; cool 10 minutes.

3 Preheat oven to 200°C/180°C fan-forced. Oil four holes of six-hole (¾-cup/180ml) texas muffin pan.

4 Cut two 13cm rounds from opposite corners of each pastry sheet; cut two 9cm rounds from remaining corners of each sheet. Place larger rounds in pan holes to cover bases and sides; trim any excess pastry, prick bases with fork.

5 Spoon lamb mixture into pastry cases; brush around edges with a little egg. Top pies with smaller rounds; gently press around edges to seal. Brush pies with remaining egg; press one rosemary sprig into top of each pie.

6 Bake pies, uncovered, about 15 minutes or until browned lightly. Stand in pan 5 minutes before serving.

7 Meanwhile, heat butter in medium saucepan; cook peas, juice and the water, uncovered, stirring occasionally, about 5 minutes or until peas are just tender.

8 Serve pies with peas.

prep + cook time 40 minutes **serves** 4
nutritional count per serving 42.7g total fat (18.6g saturated fat); 2868kJ (686 cal); 40.4g carbohydrate; 33.1g protein; 6.1g fibre

veal goulash and potato pies

¼ cup (60ml) olive oil
1kg boneless veal shoulder, cut into 2cm pieces
1 large brown onion (200g), chopped coarsely
1 large red capsicum (350g), chopped coarsely
1 clove garlic, crushed
1 tablespoon plain flour
2 teaspoons hot paprika
2 teaspoons sweet paprika
2 teaspoons caraway seeds
2 cups (500ml) beef stock
400g can diced tomatoes
1 tablespoon tomato paste
4 medium potatoes (800g), chopped coarsely
1 cup (120g) coarsely grated cheddar cheese

1 Heat 1 tablespoon of the oil in large saucepan; cook veal, in batches, until browned. Remove from pan.
2 Heat remaining oil in same pan; cook onion, capsicum and garlic, stirring, until onion softens. Add flour, spices and seeds; cook, stirring, 2 minutes.
3 Return veal to pan with stock, undrained tomatoes and paste; bring to the boil. Reduce heat; simmer, covered, 1 hour. Uncover; simmer about 30 minutes or until veal is tender and sauce thickens slightly.
4 Meanwhile, boil, steam or microwave potato until tender; drain. Mash potato in medium bowl until smooth.
5 Preheat grill.
6 Divide goulash mixture among six oiled 1¼-cup (310ml) ovenproof dishes; top with potato, sprinkle with cheese. Grill until browned.

prep + cook time 1 hour 45 minutes **makes** 6
nutritional count per pie 20.6g total fat (6.8g saturated fat);
2011kJ (481 cal); 23g carbohydrate; 48.8g protein; 3.9g fibre

chunky beef and vegetable pie

1 tablespoon olive oil
1.5kg gravy beef,
    cut into 2cm pieces
60g butter
1 medium brown onion (150g),
    chopped finely
1 clove garlic, crushed
¼ cup (35g) plain flour
1 cup (250ml) dry white wine
3 cups (750ml) hot beef stock
2 tablespoons tomato paste
2 stalks celery (200g), trimmed,
    cut into 2cm pieces

2 medium potatoes (400g),
    cut into 2cm pieces
1 large carrot (180g),
    cut into 2cm pieces
1 large zucchini (150g),
    cut into 2cm pieces
150g mushrooms, quartered
1 cup (120g) frozen peas
½ cup finely chopped fresh
    flat-leaf parsley
2 sheets puff pastry
1 egg, beaten lightly

1 Heat oil in large saucepan; cook beef, in batches, until browned all over. Remove from pan.
2 Melt butter in same pan; cook onion and garlic, stirring, until onion softens. Add flour; cook, stirring, until mixture thickens and bubbles. Gradually stir in wine and stock; stir until mixture boils and thickens slightly.
3 Return beef to pan with paste, celery, potato and carrot; bring to the boil. Reduce heat; simmer, covered, 1 hour.
4 Add zucchini and mushrooms; simmer, uncovered, about 30 minutes or until beef is tender. Add peas; stir until heated through. Remove from heat; stir in parsley.
5 Preheat oven to 220°C/200°C fan-forced.
6 Divide warm beef mixture between two deep 25cm pie dishes; brush outside edge of dishes with a little egg. Top each pie with a pastry sheet; pressing edges to seal. Trim pastry; brush pastry with egg.
7 Bake about 20 minutes or until browned.

prep + cook time 2 hours 20 minutes **serves** 8
nutritional count per serving 27.6g total fat (13.3g saturated fat); 2412kJ (577 cal); 28.6g carbohydrate; 46.4g protein; 4.9g fibre

mini beef and guinness pies

1 tablespoon vegetable oil
500g beef skirt steak, chopped finely
1 medium brown onion (150g), chopped finely
2 tablespoons plain flour
375ml bottle guinness stout
1 cup (250ml) beef stock
5 sheets shortcrust pastry
1 egg, beaten lightly

1 Heat oil in large saucepan; cook beef, stirring, until browned.
Add onion; cook, stirring, until softened. Add flour; cook, stirring,
until mixture bubbles and is well browned.
2 Gradually add stout and stock, stirring until gravy boils and thickens.
Cover, reduce heat; simmer, stirring occasionally, 1 hour. Uncover;
simmer, stirring occasionally, 30 minutes. Cool filling 10 minutes then
refrigerate until cold.
3 Preheat oven to 220°C/200°C fan-forced. Grease three 12-hole mini
(1 tablespoon/20ml) muffin pans.
4 Using 6cm pastry cutter, cut 36 rounds from pastry sheets; place
one round in each of the muffin pan holes. Using 5cm pastry cutter,
cut 36 rounds from remaining pastry sheets.
5 Spoon a heaped teaspoon of the cold filling into each pastry case;
brush around edges with egg. Top each pie with smaller pastry round,
press gently around edge to seal; brush with remaining egg. Using sharp
knife, make two small slits in top of each pie.
6 Bake pies about 15 minutes or until browned lightly. Stand 5 minutes
in pan before placing on serving platters.

prep + cook time 2 hours (+ refrigeration) **makes** 36
nutritional count per pie 7.4g total fat (3.6g saturated fat);
564kJ (135 cal); 11.3g carbohydrate; 5.1g protein; 0.5g fibre

curried chicken pies

1.6kg chicken
90g butter
1 small leek (200g), chopped finely
1 medium white onion (150g), chopped finely
1 medium red capsicum (200g), chopped finely
2 stalks celery (300g), trimmed, chopped finely
3 teaspoons curry powder
¼ teaspoon chilli powder
¼ cup (35g) plain flour
⅓ cup (80g) sour cream
½ cup finely chopped fresh flat-leaf parsley
2 sheets puff pastry
1 egg, beaten lightly

1 Place chicken in large saucepan, add enough water to just cover chicken; bring to the boil, reduce heat, simmer, uncovered, 1 hour. Remove from heat; when cool enough to handle, remove from stock. Reserve 1¾ cups of the stock for this recipe.
2 Preheat oven to 200°C/180°C fan-forced.
3 Remove skin and bones from chicken; chop chicken flesh roughly.
4 Heat butter in large frying pan; cook leek, onion, capsicum and celery, stirring, until vegetables are soft.
5 Add curry powder and chilli powder; cook, stirring, until fragrant. Stir in flour. Add reserved stock, stir over heat until mixture boils and thickens. Reduce heat; simmer 1 minute. Remove from heat. Stir in sour cream, chicken and parsley. Spoon chicken mixture into six 1¼-cup (310ml) ovenproof dishes.
6 Cut pastry into six rounds large enough to cover top of each dish. Lightly brush pastry with egg. Place pies on oven tray.
7 Bake pies 10 minutes. Reduce oven to 180°C/160°C fan-forced; bake further 15 minutes or until pastry is golden brown.

prep + cook time 2 hours (+ standing) **makes** 6
nutritional count per pie 52.8g total fat (25.4g saturated fat); 3001kJ (718 cal); 28.5g carbohydrate; 33.3g protein; 3g fibre

beef pies with polenta tops

500g beef chuck steak,
 cut into 4cm pieces
1 tablespoon plain flour
2 tablespoons olive oil
1 small onion (80g), chopped
2 cloves garlic, crushed
100g button mushrooms, halved
½ cup (125ml) dry red wine
½ cup (125ml) beef stock
1 cup (280g) canned crushed
 tomatoes
1 small red capsicum (150g),
 chopped coarsely
¼ cup (35g) coarsely chopped,
 drained sun-dried tomatoes in oil

¼ cup (40g) seeded black olives
⅓ cup chopped fresh basil
1 large potato (300g), chopped
20g butter
1 tablespoon milk
2 sheets shortcrust pastry
¼ cup (20g) finely grated
 parmesan cheese

soft polenta
¼ cup (60ml) chicken stock
¾ cup (180ml) milk
¼ cup (40g) polenta
¼ cup (20g) finely grated
 parmesan cheese

1 Coat beef in flour; shake off excess. Heat half the oil in large saucepan; cook beef, in batches, until browned. Remove from pan.

2 Heat remaining oil in same pan; cook onion, garlic and mushrooms, stirring, until vegetables soften. Add wine; bring to the boil. Return beef to pan with stock and crushed tomatoes; bring to the boil. Reduce heat; simmer, covered, 1 hour. Uncover, stir in capsicum, sun-dried tomato and olives; simmer 15 minutes or until sauce thickens; cool. Stir in basil.

3 Preheat oven to 180°C/160°C fan-forced. Oil six-hole (¾ cup/180ml) texas muffin pan.

4 Make soft polenta.

5 Meanwhile, boil, steam or microwave potato until tender; drain. Mash potato with butter and milk in medium bowl until smooth.

6 Gently swirl hot polenta mixture into hot potato mixture.

7 Cut six 12cm rounds from shortcrust pastry; press into pan holes. Spoon beef mixture into pastry cases; top with polenta mixture, sprinkle with cheese.

8 Bake pies about 30 minutes. Stand in pan 5 minutes before serving.

soft polenta Bring stock and milk to the boil in small saucepan; stir in polenta. Reduce heat; cook, stirring, 5 minutes or until thickened. Stir in cheese.

prep + cook time 2 hours 20 minutes **makes** 6
nutritional count per pie 32.3g total fat (14.6g saturated fat); 2533kJ (606 cal); 44.8g carbohydrate; 28.6g protein; 4.5g fibre

thai chicken curry pies

2 tablespoons peanut oil
1 medium brown onion (150g),
    sliced thinly
1 clove garlic, crushed
10cm stick fresh lemon grass
    (20g), chopped finely
2cm piece fresh ginger (10g),
    grated
600g chicken thigh fillets,
    cut into 3cm pieces
1 teaspoon ground cumin
½ teaspoon ground turmeric
165ml can coconut milk
1 tablespoon cornflour

¼ cup (60ml) chicken stock
1 tablespoon fish sauce
1 fresh kaffir lime leaf,
    shredded finely
1 fresh long red chilli, sliced thinly
¼ cup coarsely chopped
    fresh coriander
2 sheets shortcrust pastry
1 egg, beaten lightly
2 sheets puff pastry

1 Heat oil in large saucepan; cook onion, garlic, lemon grass and ginger, stirring, until onion softens. Add chicken; cook, stirring, until browned. Add spices; cook, stirring, until fragrant. Add coconut milk; bring to the boil. Reduce heat; simmer, uncovered, 10 minutes. Add blended cornflour and stock; cook, stirring, until mixture boils and thickens; cool. Stir in sauce, lime leaf, chilli and coriander.
2 Preheat oven to 200°C/180°C fan-forced. Grease six-hole (¾-cup/ 180ml) texas muffin pan.
3 Cut six 12cm rounds from shortcrust pastry; press into pan holes. Brush edges with a little of the egg. Spoon chicken mixture into pastry cases.
4 Cut six 9cm rounds from puff pastry; top chicken mixture with puff pastry rounds. Press edges firmly to seal. Brush tops with remaining egg. Cut a small slit in top of each pie.
5 Bake pies about 25 minutes. Stand in pan 5 minutes before serving.

prep + cook time 1 hour **makes** 6
nutritional count per pie 45.4g total fat (21.4g saturated fat); 3005kJ (719 cal); 49.6g carbohydrate; 27.7g protein; 2.3g fibre

fish chowder pies

40g butter
1 medium brown onion (150g), chopped coarsely
1 clove garlic, crushed
3 rindless bacon rashers (195g), chopped coarsely
2 tablespoons plain flour
1 cup (250ml) milk
½ cup (125ml) cream
2 small potatoes (240g), cut into 1cm pieces
600g firm white fish fillets, cut into 2cm pieces
¼ cup finely chopped fresh chives
2 sheets shortcrust pastry
1 egg, beaten lightly
2 sheets puff pastry

1 Melt butter in large saucepan; cook onion, garlic and bacon, stirring, until onion softens.
2 Add flour; cook, stirring, 1 minute. Gradually stir in combined milk and cream; bring to the boil. Add potato; simmer, covered, stirring occasionally, 8 minutes. Add fish; simmer, uncovered, 2 minutes; cool. Stir in chives.
3 Preheat oven to 200°C/180°C fan-forced. Grease six-hole (¾-cup/ 180ml) texas muffin pan.
4 Cut six 12cm rounds from shortcrust pastry; press into pan holes. Brush edges with a little of the egg. Spoon fish chowder into pastry cases.
5 Cut six 9cm rounds from puff pastry; top chowder with puff pastry rounds. Press edges firmly to seal; brush tops with remaining egg. Cut a small slit in top of each pie.
6 Bake pies about 25 minutes. Stand in pan 5 minutes before serving, top-side up, sprinkled with chopped fresh chives.

prep + cook time 1 hour **makes** 6
nutritional count per pie 51.5g total fat (28g saturated fat); 3519kJ (842 cal); 60g carbohydrate; 37.9g protein; 2.9g fibre

fetta and spinach fillo bundles

350g spinach, trimmed
1 tablespoon olive oil
1 medium brown onion (150g), chopped finely
2 cloves garlic, crushed
½ teaspoon ground nutmeg
150g fetta cheese, crumbled
3 eggs
2 teaspoons finely grated lemon rind
¼ cup coarsely chopped fresh mint
2 tablespoons finely chopped fresh dill
80g butter, melted
6 sheets fillo pastry

1 Boil, steam or microwave spinach until wilted; drain. Refresh in cold water; drain. Squeeze out excess moisture. Chop spinach coarsely; spread out on absorbent paper.
2 Heat oil in small frying pan; cook onion and garlic, stirring, until onion softens. Add nutmeg; cook, stirring, until fragrant. Cool. Combine onion mixture and spinach in medium bowl with cheese, eggs, rind and herbs.
3 Preheat oven to 200°C/180°C fan-forced. Brush six-hole (¾-cup/ 180ml) texas muffin pan with a little of the butter.
4 Brush each sheet of fillo with melted butter; fold in half to enclose buttered side. Gently press one sheet into each pan hole. Spoon spinach mixture into pastry cases; fold fillo over filling to enclose. Brush with butter.
5 Bake fillo bundles about 15 minutes. Turn bundles out, top-side up, onto baking-paper-lined oven tray; bake further 5 minutes or until browned lightly. Stand 5 minutes before serving, top-side up.

prep + cook time 40 minutes **makes** 6
nutritional count per bundle 22.9g total fat (12.3g saturated fat); 1200kJ (287 cal); 9.6g carbohydrate; 10.4g protein; 1.8g fibre

lamb masala pies with raita

2 tablespoons vegetable oil
1 medium brown onion (150g), chopped finely
600g diced lamb
⅓ cup (100g) tikka masala paste
400g can diced tomatoes
¼ cup (60ml) water
½ cup (125ml) cream
¼ cup coarsely chopped fresh coriander
2 sheets shortcrust pastry
1 egg, beaten lightly
2 sheets puff pastry
raita
¾ cup (200g) yogurt
1 lebanese cucumber (130g), seeded, chopped finely
2 tablespoons finely chopped fresh mint

1 Heat oil in large saucepan; cook onion, stirring, until onion softens. Add lamb; cook, stirring, until browned. Add paste; cook, stirring, until fragrant. Add undrained tomatoes, the water and cream; bring to the boil. Reduce heat; simmer, uncovered, about 25 minutes or until sauce thickens; cool. Stir in coriander.
2 Preheat oven to 200°C/180°C fan-forced. Grease six-hole (¾-cup/ 180ml) texas muffin pan.
3 Cut six 12cm rounds from shortcrust pastry; press into pan holes. Brush edges with a little of the egg. Spoon lamb mixture into pastry cases.
4 Cut six 9cm rounds from puff pastry; top lamb mixture with puff pastry rounds. Press edges firmly to seal; brush tops with remaining egg. Cut a small slit in top of each pie.
5 Bake pies about 25 minutes. Stand in pan 5 minutes before serving.
6 Meanwhile, make raita by combining ingredients in small bowl.
7 Sprinkle lamb masala pies with fresh coriander leaves; serve with raita.

prep + cook time 1 hour 15 minutes **makes** 6
nutritional count per pie 54g total fat (24.7g saturated fat); 3469kJ (830 cal); 52g carbohydrate; 32.3g protein; 5.1g fibre

veal goulash pies

600g diced veal shoulder
2 tablespoons plain flour
1 tablespoon sweet paprika
¼ teaspoon cayenne pepper
¼ cup (60ml) olive oil
1 small brown onion (80g),
   chopped finely
1 clove garlic, crushed
2 teaspoons caraway seeds
400g can diced tomatoes
¼ cup (60ml) beef stock

1 medium red capsicum (200g),
   cut into 2cm pieces
1 medium unpeeled potato (200g),
   cut into 2cm pieces
¼ cup (60g) sour cream
¼ cup coarsely chopped fresh
   flat-leaf parsley
2 sheets shortcrust pastry
1 egg, beaten lightly
2 sheets puff pastry

1 Coat veal in combined flour, paprika and pepper; shake off excess. Heat 2 tablespoons of the oil in large saucepan; cook veal, in batches, until browned. Remove from pan.

2 Heat remaining oil in same pan; cook onion and garlic, stirring, until onion softens. Return veal to pan with seeds, undrained tomatoes and stock; bring to the boil. Reduce heat; simmer, covered, 25 minutes. Add capsicum and potato; simmer, uncovered, about 15 minutes or until sauce thickens. Stir in sour cream and parsley; cool.

3 Preheat oven to 200°C/180°C fan-forced. Grease six-hole (¾-cup/180ml) texas muffin pan.

4 Cut six 12cm rounds from shortcrust pastry; press into pan holes. Brush edges with a little of the egg. Spoon goulash into pastry cases.

5 Cut six 9cm rounds from puff pastry; top goulash with puff pastry rounds. Press edges firmly to seal; brush tops with remaining egg. Cut a small slit in top of each pie.

6 Bake pies about 25 minutes. Stand in pan 5 minutes before serving.

prep + cook time 1 hour 15 minutes **makes** 6
nutritional count per pie 44.6g total fat (19.7g saturated fat); 3198kJ (765 cal); 56g carbohydrate; 33.3g protein; 4.1g fibre

beef and onion party pies

1 tablespoon vegetable oil
1 medium brown onion (150g), chopped finely
450g beef mince
2 tablespoons tomato paste
2 tablespoons worcestershire sauce
2 tablespoons powdered gravy mix
¾ cup (180ml) water
3 sheets shortcrust pastry
1 egg, beaten lightly
2 sheets puff pastry

1 Heat oil in large frying pan; cook onion, stirring, until onion softens. Add mince; cook, stirring, until mince changes colour. Add paste, sauce, and blended gravy powder and the water; bring to the boil, stirring. Reduce heat; simmer, uncovered, about 10 minutes or until thickened slightly; cool.
2 Preheat oven to 200°C/180°C fan-forced. Grease two 12-hole (2 tablespoons/40ml) deep flat-based patty pans.
3 Cut 24 x 7cm rounds from shortcrust pastry; press into pan holes. Spoon beef mixture into pastry cases. Brush edges with a little of the egg.
4 Cut 24 x 6cm rounds from puff pastry; top pies with puff pastry lids. Press edges firmly to seal; brush lids with remaining egg. Cut a small slit in top of each pie.
5 Bake pies about 20 minutes or until browned lightly. Stand in pan 5 minutes before serving.

prep + cook time 45 minutes **makes** 24
nutritional count per pie 11.2g total fat (5.4g saturated fat); 790kJ (189 cal); 15.5g carbohydrate; 6.4g protein; 0.7g fibre

chicken and mushroom party pies

1 tablespoon olive oil
1 small brown onion (80g), chopped finely
1 clove garlic, crushed
400g chicken mince
100g mushrooms, chopped finely
2 teaspoons plain flour
¾ cup (180ml) cream
2 tablespoons finely chopped fresh chives
3 sheets shortcrust pastry
1 egg, beaten lightly
2 sheets puff pastry
2 teaspoons sesame seeds

1 Heat oil in medium frying pan; cook onion and garlic, stirring, until onion softens. Add chicken mince and mushrooms; cook, stirring, until mince changes colour. Add flour; cook, stirring, 1 minute. Gradually stir in cream; cook, stirring, until mixture boils and thickens. Stir in chives; cool.
2 Preheat oven to 200°C/180°C fan-forced. Grease two 12-hole (2 tablespoons/40ml) deep flat-based patty pans.
3 Cut 24 x 7cm rounds from shortcrust pastry; press into pan holes. Brush edges with a little of the egg. Spoon chicken mixture into pastry cases.
4 Cut 24 x 6cm rounds from puff pastry; top pies with puff pastry lids. Press edges firmly to seal; brush lids with remaining egg, sprinkle with sesame seeds. Cut a small slit in top of each pie.
5 Bake pies about 20 minutes or until browned lightly. Stand in pan 5 minutes before serving.

prep + cook time 45 minutes **makes** 24
nutritional count per pie 14.5g total fat (7.4g saturated fat); 895kJ (214 cal); 14.8g carbohydrate; 6g protein; 0.8g fibre
tip We used chicken breast mince for this recipe.

moroccan lamb party pies

1 tablespoon vegetable oil
1 small brown onion (80g), chopped finely
1 clove garlic, crushed
400g lamb mince
2 teaspoons ground cumin
1 cup (280g) undrained canned crushed tomatoes
¼ cup (40g) roasted pine nuts
2 tablespoons finely chopped raisins
2 tablespoons finely chopped fresh coriander
3 sheets shortcrust pastry
1 egg, beaten lightly
2 sheets puff pastry

1 Heat oil in medium frying pan; cook onion and garlic, stirring, until onion softens. Add lamb; cook, stirring, until lamb changes colour. Add cumin; cook, stirring, until fragrant. Add tomatoes; bring to the boil. Reduce heat; simmer, uncovered, about 5 minutes or until thickened slightly. Stir in nuts, raisins and coriander; cool.
2 Preheat oven to 200°C/180°C fan-forced. Grease two 12-hole (2 tablespoons/40ml) deep flat-based patty pans.
3 Cut 24 x 7cm rounds from shortcrust pastry; press into pan holes. Brush edges with a little of the egg. Spoon lamb mixture into pastry cases.
4 Cut 24 x 6cm rounds from puff pastry; top pies with puff pastry lids. Press edges firmly to seal; brush lids with egg. Cut a small slit in top of each pie.
5 Bake pies about 20 minutes or until browned lightly. Stand in pan 5 minutes before serving. Serve with mango chutney, if you like.

prep + cook time 45 minutes **makes** 24
nutritional count per pie 12.2g total fat (5.5g saturated fat); 828kJ (198 cal); 15.6g carbohydrate; 6.2g protein; 0.9g fibre

beef carbonade pies

2kg beef round steak, diced into 3cm pieces
½ cup (75g) plain flour
40g butter, melted
¼ cup (60ml) vegetable oil
4 medium brown onions (600g), sliced thickly
2 large carrots (360g), chopped coarsely
2 cloves garlic, crushed
2¾ cups (680ml) stout
2 tablespoons brown sugar
¼ cup (60ml) cider vinegar
3 sprigs fresh thyme
1 bay leaf
3 sheets puff pastry
1 tablespoon milk
1 egg, beaten lightly

1 Coat beef in flour; shake off excess. Heat butter and 2 tablespoons of the oil in large deep saucepan; cook beef, in batches, until browned all over. Remove from pan.
2 Heat remaining oil in same pan; cook onion, carrot and garlic, stirring, until onion softens. Return beef to pan with stout, sugar, vinegar, thyme and bay leaf; bring to the boil. Reduce heat; simmer, covered, 1½ hours.
3 Uncover; simmer, stirring occasionally, about 1 hour or until beef is tender and sauce thickens. Discard herbs.
4 Preheat oven to 220°C/200°C fan-forced.
5 Spoon beef mixture into six 1¾-cup (430ml) ovenproof dishes. Cut each pastry sheet into two pieces, large enough to top each dish. Brush pastry with combined milk and egg; place dishes on oven tray.
6 Bake pies about 15 minutes or until pastry is puffed and browned lightly.

prep + cook time 3 hours **serves** 6
nutritional count per serving 33.9g total fat (14.4g saturated fat);
2930kJ (701 cal); 32.4g carbohydrate; 58.2g protein; 3.1g fibre

moroccan-spiced chunky lamb pies

2 tablespoons olive oil
2 medium red onions (340g),
  cut into thin wedges
4 cloves garlic, crushed
2 tablespoons plain flour
1 tablespoon ground cumin
2 teaspoons sweet paprika
2 teaspoons ground cinnamon
1.5kg trimmed diced lamb shoulder
1 litre (4 cups) chicken stock
400g can diced tomatoes
2 medium kumara (800g),
  cut into 2cm pieces

12 sheets fillo pastry
50g butter, melted
1 tablespoon icing sugar
¼ teaspoon ground cinnamon
2 teaspoons finely grated
  lemon rind
2 tablespoons lemon juice
1¼ cups (150g) seeded
  green olives, halved
½ cup finely chopped fresh
  coriander
¾ cup (200g) greek-style yogurt

1 Preheat oven to 160°C/140°C fan-forced.

2 Heat half the oil in large flameproof dish; cook onion, stirring, until softened. Add garlic; cook, stirring, until fragrant. Transfer to small bowl.

3 Combine flour, cumin, paprika and cinnamon in large bowl with lamb; shake off excess. Heat remaining oil in same dish; cook lamb, in batches, until browned. Remove from dish.

4 Add stock and undrained tomatoes to same dish; bring to the boil, stirring. Return onion mixture and lamb to dish; bring to the boil. Cover dish, transfer to oven; cook lamb 1 hour. Add kumara; cook, uncovered, further 30 minutes or until tender.

5 Increase oven to 200°C/180°C fan-forced.

6 Meanwhile, layer six sheets of fillo, brushing melted butter between each sheet; repeat with remaining fillo and most of the remaining butter. Using top of 2-cup (500ml) ovenproof dish as a guide, cut out six lids for pies, allowing about a 4cm overhang. Brush lids with any remaining butter; dust with combined icing sugar and cinnamon.

7 Skim surface of lamb mixture to remove any fat; stir in rind, juice, olives and coriander. Spoon mixture into six 2-cup (500ml) ovenproof dishes; top each dish with pastry round, folding in overhanging edge. Place dishes on oven tray; bake about 20 minutes. Serve pies with yogurt.

prep + cook time 2 hours **serves** 6
nutritional count per serving 39.5g total fat (17.7g saturated fat); 3336kJ (798 cal); 49.4g carbohydrate; 59.1g protein; 5.2g fibre

mini cottage pies

3 medium potatoes (600g), chopped coarsely
1 tablespoon olive oil
1 medium brown onion (150g), chopped finely
2 cloves garlic, crushed
250g beef mince
1 cup (250ml) tomato puree
⅓ cup (80ml) dry red wine
2 tablespoons worcestershire sauce
1 tablespoon fresh thyme leaves
¼ cup (30g) frozen peas
2 tablespoons finely chopped fresh flat-leaf parsley
¼ cup (60g) sour cream
1 egg yolk
48 x 4cm tartlet cases

1 Boil, steam or microwave potato until tender; drain.
2 Meanwhile, heat oil in large frying pan; cook onion and garlic until onion softens. Add mince; cook, stirring, until mince changes colour. Stir in puree, wine, sauce and thyme; bring to the boil. Reduce heat; simmer, uncovered, about 15 minutes or until almost all liquid has evaporated. Stir in peas and parsley.
3 Mash potato in large bowl with sour cream and egg yolk until combined. Spoon potato mixture into piping bag fitted with large fluted tube.
4 Preheat grill.
5 Place pastry cases on oven trays. Spoon beef mixture into cases; pipe potato over beef. Grill pies about 5 minutes or until tops brown and pies are heated through.

prep + cook time 45 minutes **makes** 48
nutritional count per pie 4.3g total fat (2.2g saturated fat); 322kJ (77 cal); 6.8g carbohydrate; 2.3g protein; 0.6g fibre
tip You need to purchase 48 baked 4cm tartlet cases for this recipe.

herbed veal and tomato pie

2½ cups (375g) plain flour
200g cold butter, chopped
3 egg yolks
2 tablespoons iced water
filling
¼ cup (60ml) olive oil
8 baby onions (200g), halved
1kg diced veal
¼ cup (35g) plain flour

2 x 425g cans tomatoes
2 tablespoons tomato paste
¼ cup (60ml) dry red wine
2 tablespoons coarsely chopped
  fresh oregano
1 tablespoon chopped fresh thyme
250g button mushrooms
2 tablespoons plain flour, extra
2 tablespoons water

1 Sift flour into bowl; rub in butter. Add 2 of the egg yolks and enough of the water to make ingredients cling together. Press dough into a ball; knead gently on floured surface until smooth. Wrap in plastic; refrigerate 30 minutes.

2 Meanwhile, make filling.

3 Preheat oven to 200°C/180°C fan-forced.

4 Roll two-thirds of the pastry between sheets of baking paper until large enough to line 24cm round pie dish (2 litre/8 cup). Lift pastry into dish; ease into side, trim edge. Line pastry with baking paper, fill with dried beans or rice; place on oven tray. Bake 10 minutes. Remove paper and beans; bake further 10 minutes or until browned lightly. Cool.

5 Increase oven to 220°C/200°C fan-forced.

6 Roll remaining pastry and scraps until 3mm thick. Fill pastry case with filling, top with pastry; cut a square of pastry from the centre. Brush with a little of the remaining egg yolk. Bake about 40 minutes or until lightly browned and heated through.

filling Heat 1 tablespoon of the oil in pan; cook onions, stirring, until browned. Drain. Toss veal in flour, shake away excess flour. Heat remaining oil in pan; cook veal, in batches, until browned all over. Remove veal from pan. Add undrained crushed tomatoes, paste and wine to same pan; cook, stirring, until mixture boils and thickens. Add herbs. Return veal to pan; simmer, uncovered, 30 minutes, stirring occasionally. Add onions and mushrooms; cook 15 minutes or until veal is tender. Stir in blended extra flour and water, stir over heat until mixture boils and thickens. Cool.

prep + cook time 3 hours **serves** 6
nutritional count per serving 42.8g total fat (21.2g saturated fat); 3582kJ (857 cal); 61.5g carbohydrate; 51.4g protein; 6.6g fibre

zucchini, pea and fontina pasties

2 teaspoons olive oil
1 small brown onion (100g),
  chopped finely
2 medium zucchini (240g),
  grated coarsely
¾ cup (90g) frozen peas, thawed
¼ cup lightly packed fresh
  mint leaves, sliced finely
100g fontina cheese,
  cut into 5mm cubes

1 teaspoon finely grated
  lemon rind
1 egg yolk
1 tablespoon milk
hot water pastry
¾ cup (180ml) water
125g butter, chopped coarsely
3 cups (450g) plain flour
1 teaspoon salt
1 egg yolk

1 Preheat oven to 200°C/180°C fan-forced. Grease oven trays.

2 Heat oil in large frying pan; cook onion and zucchini over high heat until vegetables soften slightly. Cool.

3 Stir peas, mint, cheese and rind into zucchini mixture.

4 Make hot water pastry.

5 Cut pastry in half, return one half to same bowl; cover with tea towel to keep warm. Roll other half of pastry as thinly as possible, on a floured surface into a round about 50cm in diameter.

6 Working quickly, cut out 8cm rounds from pastry, cover pastry with tea towel to prevent drying out while shaping each pasty. Place a rounded teaspoon of filling on each pastry round, fold in half and press edges together firmly. Place pasties on trays; brush with combined egg yolk and milk.

7 Bake pasties about 25 minutes or until golden brown. Serve warm with minted yogurt.

hot water pastry Bring the water and butter to the boil in small saucepan. Meanwhile, sift flour and salt into large bowl. Make a well in the centre, add egg yolk; cover yolk with some of the flour. Pour boiling water mixture over flour, stirring constantly with a knife until ingredients are combined. Knead pastry lightly and quickly on floured surface until smooth. Place pastry in bowl, cover with tea towel to keep warm.

prep + cook time 1 hour **makes** 60
nutritional count per pastry 2.7g total fat (1.5g saturated fat); 226kJ (54 cal); 5.7g carbohydrate; 1.5g protein; 0.5g fibre

egg and bacon pie

2 cups (320g) wholemeal
plain flour
1 cup (150g) white plain flour
200g cold butter, chopped
1 egg
2 tablespoons iced water,
approximately
2 teaspoons olive oil
1 large onion (200g), chopped

10 rindless bacon rashers (650g),
chopped
8 eggs, extra
2 cups (250g) grated tasty
cheddar cheese
½ teaspoon seasoned pepper
¼ cup chopped fresh chives
1 egg yolk

1 Grease deep 25cm round pie dish. Sift flours into bowl, rub in butter
(or process flours and butter until mixture resembles breadcrumbs). Add
egg and enough water to make ingredients cling together (or process
until ingredients just come together). Press dough into a ball, knead on
floured surface until smooth. Wrap in plastic; refrigerate 30 minutes.
2 Roll two-thirds of the pastry between sheets of baking paper until
large enough to line dish. Lift pastry carefully into dish; ease into side,
trim edge. Prick base with fork; cover, refrigerate 30 minutes.
3 Preheat oven to 200°C/180°C fan-forced.
4 Line pastry with baking paper, fill with dried beans or rice; place on
oven tray. Bake 10 minutes. Remove paper and beans; bake further
10 minutes or until browned. Cool.
5 Reduce oven to 180°C/160°C fan-forced.
6 Heat oil in medium frying pan; cook onion and bacon, stirring, until
onion is soft.
7 Break an extra egg into a cup, gently pour unbeaten egg into pastry
case. Repeat with remaining eggs. Top with bacon mixture and combined
cheese, pepper and chives.
8 Roll remaining pastry until large enough to cover pie. Brush edge
of pie with egg yolk, carefully lift pastry onto pie; trim edge carefully.
9 Bake pie about 45 minutes or until browned.

prep + cook time 1 hour 30 minutes (+ refrigeration) **serves** 6
nutritional count per serving 57.5g total fat (31.6g saturated fat);
3816kJ (913 cal); 51.7g carbohydrate; 44.9g protein; 7g fibre

caraway, potato and mushroom mini pies

1½ cups (225g) plain flour
¾ cup (105g) self-raising flour
1½ teaspoons caraway seeds
50g cold butter, chopped
1 egg yolk
1 egg, beaten lightly
⅓ cup (80ml) iced water,
    approximately
filling
10 baby new potatoes (400g),
    quartered
60g butter

2 medium brown onions (300g),
    sliced
1 teaspoon caraway seeds
150g button mushrooms,
    chopped coarsely
¼ cup (35g) plain flour
1½ cups (375ml) vegetable stock
1 teaspoon dijon mustard
1 tablespoon chopped
    fresh rosemary
⅓ cup (25g) grated parmesan
    cheese

1 Sift flours into large bowl, add seeds; rub in butter. Add egg yolk,
egg and enough water to make ingredients cling together. Press
dough into a ball, knead on floured surface until smooth. Wrap in plastic;
refrigerate 30 minutes.
2 Meanwhile, make filling.
3 Preheat oven to 240°C/220°C fan-forced. Grease four holes of texas
(¾-cup/180ml) muffin pan.
4 Divide two-thirds of the pastry into four portions. Roll each portion on
floured surface until 2mm thick, line pan holes, trim so pastry overhangs
by 1cm. Brush overhanging edges with egg. Divide filling between cases.
5 Roll out remaining pastry, cut into four 12cm rounds; place over filling,
pinch edges together. Decorate with pastry shapes, if desired; brush pies
with remaining egg.
6 Bake pies 5 minutes. Reduce oven to 220°C/200°C fan-forced; bake
further 25 minutes or until pies are browned.
filling Boil, steam or microwave potatoes until just tender; drain, cool.
Heat butter in frying pan; cook onions, stirring, until soft. Add seeds and
mushrooms; cook, stirring, 5 minutes. Stir in flour over heat until bubbling.
Remove from heat, gradually stir in stock; simmer, uncovered, stirring
occasionally, about 15 minutes. Stir in mustard, rosemary, cheese and
potatoes; cool.

prep + cook time 1 hour (+ refrigeration) **makes** 4
nutritional count per pie 29g total fat (17.3g saturated fat);
2909kJ (696 cal); 84.1g carbohydrate; 20.6g protein; 7.4g fibre

spinach pies

1 tablespoon olive oil
1 large brown onion (200g), chopped finely
375g baby spinach leaves
1 teaspoon lemon rind
¼ cup (60ml) lemon juice
3 sheets puff pastry
2 tablespoons pine nuts

1 Preheat oven to 220°C/200°C fan-forced. Line oven tray with baking paper.
2 Heat oil in large frying pan; cook onion, stirring, until softened. Add half the spinach; cook, stirring, until wilted. Add remaining spinach, rind and juice; cook, stirring, until liquid has evaporated. Remove from heat; cool 5 minutes.
3 Cut 12 x 11cm rounds from pastry. Divide spinach mixture among rounds. Gather three points of each round together to form a triangle, leaving top of filling exposed. Pinch and twist each corner to secure pastry round. Place pies on oven tray; sprinkle filling with pine nuts.
4 Bake pies about 15 minutes or until pastry is browned.

prep + cook time 45 minutes **makes** 12
nutritional count per pie 11.1g total fat (5.3g saturated fat); 757kJ (181 cal); 16.3g carbohydrate; 3.4g protein; 1.6g fibre

chicken, raisin and pine nut empanadas

1 litre (4 cups) water
200g chicken breast fillet
2 teaspoons olive oil
1 small brown onion (80g),
  chopped finely
2 cloves garlic, crushed
½ can (205g) crushed tomatoes
1 bay leaf
¼ teaspoon dried chilli flakes
2 tablespoons raisins, chopped

2 tablespoons roasted pine nuts
½ teaspoon ground cinnamon
2 tablespoons finely chopped
  fresh flat-leaf parsley
1 egg
pastry
1⅔ cups (250g) plain flour
150g cold butter, chopped
1 egg
1 tablespoon cold water

1 Bring the water to the boil in medium saucepan; add chicken, return to the boil. Reduce heat; simmer, covered, about 10 minutes or until chicken is cooked through. Cool chicken in poaching liquid 10 minutes. Remove chicken from pan; discard poaching liquid. Shred chicken finely.

2 Heat oil in medium frying pan; cook onion and garlic, stirring, until onion softens. Add undrained tomato, bay leaf and chilli; cook, stirring occasionally, about 5 minutes or until mixture thickens.

3 Add chicken, raisins, nuts and cinnamon to tomato mixture; stir until heated through. Stir in parsley. Cool mixture, covered, in the refrigerator.

4 Meanwhile, make pastry.

5 Preheat oven to 200°C/180°C fan-forced.

6 Roll one pastry half between sheets of baking paper until 2mm thick; using 10cm-round cutter, cut 10 rounds from pastry. Place 1 level tablespoon of chicken mixture in centre of each round; fold round in half to enclose filling, pinching edges to seal. Press around edges with a fork. Repeat with remaining pastry half and chicken mixture to make a total of 20 empanadas, re-rolling pastry scraps as required.

7 Place empanadas on baking-paper-lined oven trays; brush with egg. Bake about 20 minutes or until browned lightly.

pastry Process flour and butter until crumbly. Add egg and the water; process until mixture comes together. Knead dough on floured surface until smooth. Halve pastry, enclose in plastic wrap; refrigerate 30 minutes.

prep + cook time 2 hours (+ refrigeration) **makes** 20
nutritional count per empanada 8.9g total fat (4.5g saturated fat); 594kJ (142 cal); 10.6g carbohydrate; 4.6g protein; 0.9g fibre

cheese pastries

1 ½ cups (225g) plain flour
1 ½ cups (225g) self-raising flour
½ teaspoon salt
¾ cup (180ml) warm water
¼ cup (60ml) olive oil
1 egg, beaten lightly
2 teaspoons sesame seeds
filling
1 egg, beaten lightly
100g fetta cheese, crumbled
½ cup (120g) ricotta cheese
½ cup (40g) finely grated romano cheese

1 Preheat oven to 200°C/180°C fan-forced. Grease oven trays; line with baking paper.
2 Process flours and salt until combined. While motor is operating, add enough of the combined water and oil so the mixture forms a ball (do not overmix). Wrap dough in plastic; refrigerate 30 minutes.
3 Meanwhile, make filling.
4 Divide dough in half. Roll each half on floured surface to 30cm x 40cm rectangle; cut 13 x 8.5cm rounds from each half. Drop rounded teaspoons of filling onto rounds; brush edges with a little water. Fold rounds in half, press edges together with a fork to seal. Place pastries on trays; brush with egg, sprinkle with seeds.
5 Bake pastries about 15 minutes or until browned lightly.
filling Combine ingredients in medium bowl.

prep + cook time 1 hour 15 minutes (+ refrigeration) **makes** 26
nutritional count per pastry 4.7g total fat (1.6g saturated fat); 456kJ (109 cal); 12.4g carbohydrate; 4g protein; 0.7g fibre
tip Parmesan cheese can be used instead of romano cheese.

gluten-free mini meat pies

2 teaspoons vegetable oil
1 medium brown onion (150g), chopped finely
2 rindless bacon rashers (130g), chopped finely
350g beef mince
2 tablespoons tomato paste
¼ cup (35g) arrowroot
2 cups (500ml) gluten-free beef stock
1 egg, beaten lightly
pastry
1¾ cups (315g) rice flour
⅓ cup (50g) (corn) cornflour
⅓ cup (40g) soya flour
200g cold butter, chopped
¼ cup (60ml) cold water, approximately

1 Heat oil in medium saucepan; cook onion and bacon, stirring, until onion softens and bacon is browned. Add beef; cook, stirring, until browned. Add paste and blended arrowroot and stock; bring to the boil, stirring. Reduce heat; simmer, uncovered, until thickened. Cool.
2 Meanwhile, make pastry.
3 Preheat oven to 220°C/200°C fan-forced. Oil 12 x ¼-cup (60ml) foil pie cases (7cm diameter top, 5cm diameter base); place on oven tray.
4 Roll pastry between sheets of baking paper until 5mm thick; cut 12 x 9cm rounds from pastry. Ease pastry rounds into cases; press into base and sides. Spoon beef mixture into pastry cases; brush edges with egg. Cut 12 x 7cm rounds from remaining pastry; place rounds on pies, press to seal edges. Brush pies with egg; cut two small slits in top of each pie.
5 Bake pies about 25 minutes. Serve with gluten-free tomato sauce.
pastry Process flours and butter until mixture is fine. Add enough of the water to make ingredients come together. Cover; refrigerate 30 minutes.

prep + cook time 1 hour (+ refrigeration and standing) **makes** 12
nutritional count per pie 19.3g total fat (11g saturated fat); 1032kJ (247 cal); 7.8g carbohydrate; 10.7g protein; 0.7g fibre
tip This recipe is also wheat-free, yeast-free and nut-free.

beef samosas with peach chutney

2 teaspoons vegetable oil
1 small brown onion (80g),
    chopped finely
2 cloves garlic, crushed
2cm piece fresh ginger (10g),
    grated
1 tablespoon ground cumin
1 tablespoon ground coriander
1 fresh small red thai chilli,
    chopped finely
250g beef mince
1 small kumara (250g),
    chopped finely
⅓ cup (80ml) water
4 sheets shortcrust pastry
1 egg, beaten lightly

peach chutney
3 medium peaches (450g)
⅓ cup (110g) raisins,
    chopped finely
½ cup (125ml) cider vinegar
2 tablespoons lemon juice
1 small brown onion (80g),
    chopped finely
¼ teaspoon ground cinnamon
½ teaspoon ground allspice
1 cup (220g) white sugar

1 Make peach chutney.
2 Heat oil in large frying pan; cook onion, garlic, ginger and spices, stirring, until onion softens. Add chilli and mince; cook, stirring, until mince browns. Add kumara and the water; bring to the boil. Reduce heat; simmer, uncovered, stirring occasionally, until kumara softens. Stir in ⅓ cup of the chutney. Cool filling 10 minutes, then refrigerate until cold.
3 Preheat oven to 200°C/180°C fan-forced. Oil three oven trays.
4 Cut nine 7.5cm rounds from each pastry sheet. Place rounded teaspoons of the filling in centre of each round; brush edges with egg, press edges together to enclose filling. Repeat process with remaining rounds and filling. Place samosas on trays; brush tops with remaining egg.
5 Bake samosas about 20 minutes or until browned lightly. Serve with remaining chutney.
peach chutney Cover peaches with boiling water in medium heatproof bowl 30 seconds. Peel, seed, then chop peaches finely. Place in medium saucepan with remaining ingredients; bring to the boil. Reduce heat; simmer, uncovered, stirring occasionally, 45 minutes or until chutney is thickened.

prep + cook time 1 hour 40 minutes (+ refrigeration) **makes** 36
nutritional count per samosa 5.7g total fat (2.8g saturated fat); 560kJ (134 cal); 17.8g carbohydrate; 3.1g protein; 0.8g fibre

SWEET PIES

quince and rhubarb pie

2 cups (500ml) water
2 cups (440g) caster sugar
4 medium quinces (1.2kg),
    peeled, quartered
2 strips lemon rind
500g rhubarb, chopped coarsely
¼ cup (60ml) lemon juice,
    approximately

1 cup (150g) plain flour
⅓ cup (55g) icing sugar
100g cold butter, chopped
1 egg, separated
1 tablespoon iced water,
    approximately
1 tablespoon raw sugar

1 Stir the water and sugar in medium saucepan over low heat until sugar has dissolved. Add quince and rind; bring to the boil. Reduce heat; simmer, covered, about 2 hours, or until quinces are tender and a rosy colour. Add rhubarb; cook 5 minutes or until rhubarb softens. Add juice to taste, to reduce sweetness. Cool quince and rhubarb in the syrup.
2 Meanwhile, process flour, icing sugar and butter until crumbly. Add egg yolk and iced water, process until ingredients just come together. Knead gently on floured surface until smooth. Cover; refrigerate 30 minutes.
3 Preheat oven to 180°C/160°C fan-forced. Grease 23cm pie dish.
4 Drain fruit mixture, reserving ⅓ cup of the syrup. Spoon fruit mixture and reserved syrup into dish.
5 Roll out pastry until large enough to cover pie. Using a 1cm cutter, cut out rounds from pastry, reserving rounds. Place pastry over filling, trim edge with a knife. Place rounds on pastry, brush a little of the lightly beaten egg white over pastry; sprinkle with raw sugar. Place pie on an oven tray.
6 Bake pie about 30 minutes or until well browned. (Cover the edges of the pastry with foil after 20 minutes to prevent over-browning). Stand 10 minutes before serving with double cream, if you like.

prep + cook time 3 hours (+ refrigeration) **serves** 8
nutritional count per serving 11.6g total fat (7g saturated fat); 2061kJ (493 cal); 90.2g carbohydrate; 4.6g protein; 9.9g fibre

rhubarb and almond jalousie

2 cups (250g) chopped rhubarb
⅓ cup (75g) caster sugar
2 sheets puff pastry
1 tablespoon apricot jam
1 egg white
1 tablespoon caster sugar, extra
frangipane filling
30g butter
¼ teaspoon vanilla extract
¼ cup (55g) caster sugar
1 egg
1 tablespoon plain flour
⅔ cup (80g) ground almonds

1 Place rhubarb and sugar in medium saucepan; cook over low heat, stirring, until sugar dissolves and rhubarb softens.
2 Preheat oven to 200°C/180°C fan-forced. Grease oven tray.
3 Make frangipane filling.
4 Cut one pastry sheet into 14cm x 24cm rectangle; cut remaining pastry sheet into 16cm x 24cm rectangle. Leaving 2cm border around all sides, make about eight evenly spaced slits across width of larger pastry piece.
5 Place smaller pastry sheet on tray; spread with jam. Place filling on pastry, leaving 2cm border around edges; top filling evenly with rhubarb mixture. Brush around border with egg white. Place remaining pastry sheet over filling; press edges of pastry together to seal. Brush jalousie with remaining egg white; sprinkle with extra sugar.
6 Bake jalousie about 35 minutes or until browned lightly and cooked through. Serve warm or cool with vanilla ice-cream, if you like.
frangipane filling Beat butter, vanilla and sugar in small bowl with electric mixer until thick and creamy. Beat in egg until combined. Stir in flour and ground almonds.

prep + cook time 1 hour **serves** 8
nutritional count per serving 18.9g total fat (3.3g saturated fat); 1446kJ (346 cal); 37.6g carbohydrate; 6.4g protein; 2.2g fibre
tip You need about 4 large trimmed stalks of rhubarb for this recipe.

blackberry and apple pie

9 medium apples (1.4kg),
   peeled, cored, sliced thickly
2 tablespoons caster sugar
1 tablespoon cornflour
1 tablespoon water
300g frozen blackberries
1 tablespoon cornflour, extra
1 egg white
1 tablespoon demerara sugar

pastry
2 cups (300g) plain flour
⅔ cup (110g) icing sugar
185g cold butter,
   chopped coarsely
2 egg yolks
1 tablespoon iced water,
   approximately

1 Make pastry.

2 Meanwhile, cook apple and caster sugar in large saucepan, covered, over low heat, about 10 minutes or until apples soften. Strain over small saucepan; reserve cooking liquid. Blend cornflour with the water; stir into reserved cooking liquid over heat until mixture boils and thickens. Place apples in large bowl, gently stir in cornflour mixture.

3 Preheat oven to 220°C/200°C fan-forced. Grease deep 23cm pie dish.

4 Roll out two-thirds of the pastry between sheets of baking paper until large enough to line dish. Ease pastry into dish; trim edge.

5 Toss blackberries in extra cornflour; stir gently into apple mixture. Spoon fruit mixture into pastry case; brush pastry edge with egg white.

6 Roll remaining pastry large enough to cover pie. Place pastry over filling; press edges together to seal. Brush pastry with egg white; sprinkle with demerara sugar. Using knife, make three cuts in top of pastry.

7 Bake pie 20 minutes. Reduce oven to 180°C/160°C fan-forced; bake 30 minutes.

pastry Process flour, sugar and butter until crumbly. Add egg yolks and enough of the water to process until ingredients come together. Knead on floured surface until smooth. Enclose in plastic wrap; refrigerate 30 minutes.

prep + cook time 1 hour 15 minutes (+ refrigeration) **serves** 8
nutritional count per serving 20.9g total fat (12.9g saturated fat); 2052kJ (491 cal); 69.1g carbohydrate; 5.8g protein; 6.3g fibre
tip We used golden delicious apples in this recipe.

apple cranberry pie

2 cups (300g) plain flour
150g butter, chopped coarsely
½ cup (125ml) iced water,
  approximately
1 egg white
1 tablespoon caster sugar

apple filling
10 medium apples (1.5kg)
½ cup (125ml) water
⅓ cup (75g) caster sugar
cranberry filling
½ cup (110g) caster sugar
2 tablespoons water
300g frozen cranberries

1 Process flour and butter until crumbly; add enough of the water to process until ingredients come together. Press dough into a smooth ball. Enclose in plastic wrap; refrigerate 1 hour.

2 Make apple filling. Make cranberry filling.

3 Preheat oven to 220°C/200°C fan-forced.

4 Roll two-thirds of the pastry between sheets of baking paper until large enough to line base of deep 25cm pie dish. Lift pastry into dish; trim edge. Spoon cranberry filling into pastry case; top with apple filling. Brush edge with egg white.

5 Roll remaining pastry until large enough to cover top of pie; press edges together. Brush with egg white; sprinkle with sugar.

6 Bake pie 15 minutes. Reduce oven to 180°C/160°C fan-forced; bake further 30 minutes.

apple filling Peel, quarter, core and slice apples thinly; combine in large saucepan with the water; simmer, stirring occasionally, about 10 minutes or until apple is tender. Drain well; transfer apples to medium bowl, stir in sugar. Cool.

cranberry filling Combine sugar, the water and cranberries in medium saucepan; simmer, stirring, about 10 minutes or until syrupy. Remove from heat; cool.

prep + cook time 1 hour 15 minutes (+ refrigeration) **serves** 8
nutritional count per serving 16.8g total fat (10.5g saturated fat); 1981kJ (474 cal); 72.2g carbohydrate; 5.7g protein; 4.9g fibre

apple pie

10 medium apples (1.5kg)
½ cup (125ml) water
¼ cup (55g) caster sugar
1 teaspoon finely grated lemon rind
¼ teaspoon ground cinnamon
1 egg white
1 tablespoon caster sugar, extra
pastry
1 cup (150g) plain flour
½ cup (75g) self-raising flour
¼ cup (35g) cornflour
¼ cup (30g) custard powder
1 tablespoon caster sugar
100g cold butter, chopped coarsely
1 egg yolk
¼ cup (60ml) iced water

1 Make pastry.
2 Peel, core and slice apple thickly. Place apple and the water in large saucepan; bring to the boil. Reduce heat; simmer, covered, 10 minutes or until apples soften. Drain; stir in sugar, rind and cinnamon. Cool.
3 Preheat oven to 220°C/200°C fan-forced. Grease deep 25cm pie dish.
4 Divide pastry in half. Roll one half between sheets of baking paper until large enough to line dish. Lift pastry into dish; press into base and side. Spoon apple mixture into pastry case; brush edge with egg white.
5 Roll remaining pastry large enough to cover filling; lift onto filling. Press edges together; trim away excess pastry. Brush pastry with egg white; sprinkle with extra sugar.
6 Bake pie 20 minutes. Reduce oven to 180°C/160°C fan-forced; bake about 25 minutes or until golden brown. Serve with vanilla custard, or scoops of vanilla ice-cream, if you like.
pastry Process dry ingredients with the butter until crumbly. Add egg yolk and the water; process until combined. Knead on floured surface until smooth. Cover; refrigerate 30 minutes.

prep + cook time 1 hour 45 minutes (+ refrigeration) **serves** 8
nutritional count per serving 11.4g total fat (7g saturated fat);
1438kJ (344 cal); 53.9g carbohydrate; 4.3g protein; 3.7g fibre

rhubarb galette

20g butter, melted
2½ cups (275g) coarsely chopped rhubarb
⅓ cup (75g) firmly packed brown sugar
1 teaspoon finely grated orange rind
1 sheet puff pastry
2 tablespoons ground hazelnuts
10g butter, melted, extra

1 Preheat oven to 220°C/200°C fan-forced. Line oven tray with baking paper.
2 Combine butter, rhubarb, sugar and rind in medium bowl.
3 Cut 24cm round from pastry, place on tray; sprinkle with ground hazelnuts. Spread rhubarb mixture over pastry, leaving 4cm border. Fold 2cm of pastry edge up and around filling. Brush edge with extra butter.
4 Bake galette 20 minutes or until browned lightly.

prep + cook time 30 minutes **serves** 4
nutritional count per serving 18.2g total fat (4.8g saturated); 1354kJ (324 cal); 34.6g carbohydrate; 4 protein; 3.2g fibre

country apple pie

1¾ cups (260g) plain flour
¼ cup (35g) self-raising flour
1 tablespoon icing sugar
125g butter, chopped
1 egg, beaten lightly
2 tablespoons lemon juice, approximately
1 egg white
2 tablespoons apricot jam
apple filling
5 large apples (1kg), sliced thinly
¼ cup (60ml) water
2 tablespoons caster sugar
1 teaspoon grated lemon rind

1 Sift flours and sugar into bowl; rub in butter. Add egg and enough juice to mix to a firm dough. Cover; refrigerate 30 minutes.
2 Meanwhile, make apple filling.
3 Grease 23cm flan tin. Roll three-quarters of the pastry between sheets of baking paper until large enough to line tin. Ease pastry into tin, press into base and side; trim edge. Cover; refrigerate 30 minutes, along with remaining pastry and any scraps.
4 Preheat oven to 200°C/180°C fan-forced.
5 Line pastry case with baking paper; fill with dried beans or rice. Bake about 7 minutes; remove paper and beans. Bake a further 7 minutes.
6 Spread cold apple filling into pastry case. Roll remaining pastry out to 3mm thickness, cut into 1cm strips. Brush edge of pastry with egg white. Place pastry strips over filling in a lattice pattern, press gently against edge of pastry, brush with egg white.
7 Bake pie about 20 minutes or until pastry is golden brown. Brush pie with warmed sieved jam.
apple filling Bring apples and the water to the boil in large saucepan. Reduce heat; simmer, covered, over low heat about 5 minutes or until apples are tender. Stir in sugar and rind; cool, drain.

prep + cook time 1 hour (+ refrigeration) **serves** 6
nutritional count per serving 18.8g total fat (11.7g saturated); 1894kJ (453 cal); 62.2g carbohydrate; 7.7g protein; 4.4g fibre

mini berry pies

300g frozen mixed berries
¼ cup (55g) caster sugar
2 teaspoons cornflour
1 tablespoon water
5 sheets shortcrust pastry
1 egg white
1 tablespoon caster sugar, extra

1 Preheat oven to 200°C/180°C fan-forced. Grease three 12-hole
(1 tablespoon/20ml) mini muffin pans.
2 Stir berries and sugar in small saucepan over heat until sugar
dissolves. Bring to the boil. Blend cornflour with the water; stir into
berry mixture. Stir over heat until mixture boils and thickens. Cool.
3 Cut 36 x 6cm rounds from pastry; press rounds into pan holes.
Cut 36 x 4cm rounds from remaining pastry. Spoon berry mixture into
pastry cases; top with rounds. Press edges firmly to seal. Brush tops with
egg white; sprinkle with extra sugar. Make small cut in top of each pie.
4 Bake pies about 20 minutes. Stand in pan 10 minutes before turning,
top-side up, onto wire rack. Serve pies warm or cold.

prep + cook time 45 minutes **makes** 36
nutritional count per pie 6.4g total fat (3.4g saturated);
489kJ (117 cal); 13g carbohydrate; 1.7g protein; 0.9g fibre

pistachio orange pie

1 ⅓ cups (185g) coarsely chopped unsalted pistachios
1 tablespoon plain flour
2 tablespoons brown sugar
40g butter, melted
2 eggs
¾ cup (180ml) maple syrup
2 teaspoons finely grated orange rind
1 tablespoon orange juice
2 tablespoons orange marmalade, warmed, sieved
pastry
1 ¼ cups (185g) plain flour
⅓ cup (55g) icing sugar
125g cold butter, chopped coarsely
1 egg yolk
1 teaspoon iced water, approximately

1 Make pastry.
2 Grease 24cm-round loose-based flan tin. Roll pastry between sheets of baking paper until large enough to line tin. Ease pastry into tin, press into base and side; trim edge. Cover; refrigerate 30 minutes.
3 Preheat oven to 180°C/160°C fan-forced.
4 Place tin on oven tray. Line pastry case with baking paper; fill with dried beans or rice. Bake 10 minutes; remove paper and beans. Bake further 5 minutes; cool.
5 Reduce oven to 160°C/140°C fan-forced.
6 Combine nuts, flour, sugar, butter, eggs, syrup, rind and juice in medium bowl. Pour mixture into pastry case.
7 Bake pie about 45 minutes. Cool. Brush pie with marmalade.
pastry Process flour, icing sugar and butter until crumbly. Add egg yolk and enough of the water to process until ingredients come together. Knead dough on floured surface until smooth. Cover; refrigerate 30 minutes.

prep + cook time 1 hour 20 minutes (+ refrigeration) **serves** 10
nutritional count per serving 23.7g total fat (10.2g saturated fat); 1785kJ (427 cal); 44.9g carbohydrate; 7.4g protein; 2.5g fibre

spiced apricot and plum pie

2 x 825g cans dark plums in light syrup
2 cups (300g) dried apricots
1 cinnamon stick
3 cloves
½ teaspoon mixed spice
½ teaspoon ground ginger
2 sheets puff pastry
1 egg, beaten lightly
spiced yogurt cream
½ cup (140g) yogurt
½ cup (120g) sour cream
1 tablespoon ground cinnamon
¼ teaspoon ground ginger
1 tablespoon icing sugar

1 Preheat oven to 200°C/180°C fan-forced. Grease 26cm pie dish or deep 1.25 litre (5-cup) rectangular dish.
2 Drain plums; reserve 1 cup of the syrup. Halve plums, discard stones, place plums in dish.
3 Place reserved syrup, apricots, cinnamon, cloves, mixed spice and ginger in medium saucepan; simmer, uncovered, until liquid is reduced to ½ cup. Remove and discard cinnamon stick and cloves; cool to room temperature. Pour mixture over plums.
4 Cut pastry into 2.5cm strips. Brush edge of dish with some of the egg; press pastry strips around edge of dish. Twist remaining strips, place over filling in a lattice pattern; trim ends, brush top with remaining egg.
5 Bake pie about 40 minutes or until pastry is browned lightly.
6 Make spiced yogurt cream.
7 Serve pie, dusted with icing sugar and spiced yogurt cream.
spiced yogurt cream Combine ingredients in small bowl.

prep + cook time 1 hour (+ cooling) **serves** 8
nutritional count per serving 16.6g total fat (5.1g saturated fat); 1935kJ (463 cal); 68.1g carbohydrate; 7g protein; 6g fibre

berry and rhubarb pies

2 cups (220g) coarsely
  chopped rhubarb
¼ cup (55g) caster sugar
2 tablespoons water
1 tablespoon cornflour
2 cups (300g) frozen mixed berries
1 egg white
2 teaspoons caster sugar, extra

pastry
1⅔ cups (250g) plain flour
⅓ cup (75g) caster sugar
150g cold butter,
  chopped coarsely
1 egg yolk

1 Make pastry.

2 Place rhubarb, sugar and half the water in medium saucepan; bring to the boil. Reduce heat; simmer, covered, about 3 minutes or until rhubarb is tender. Blend cornflour with the remaining water; stir into rhubarb mixture. Stir over heat until mixture boils and thickens. Remove from heat; stir in berries. Cool.

3 Grease six-hole (¾-cup/180ml) texas muffin pan. Roll two-thirds of the pastry between sheets of baking paper to 4mm thickness; cut out six 12cm rounds. Press rounds into pan holes. Refrigerate 30 minutes.

4 Preheat oven to 200°C/180°C fan-forced.

5 Roll remaining pastry between sheets of baking paper to 4mm thickness; cut out six 9cm rounds.

6 Spoon fruit mixture into pastry cases.

7 Brush edge of 9cm rounds with egg white; place over filling. Press edges firmly to seal. Brush tops with egg white; sprinkle with extra sugar.

8 Bake pies about 30 minutes. Stand in pan 10 minutes; using palette knife, loosen pies from edge of pan before lifting out. Serve warm with vanilla ice-cream, if you like.

pastry Process flour, sugar and butter until crumbly. Add egg yolk; process until combined. Knead on floured surface until smooth. Cover; refrigerate 30 minutes.

prep + cook time 1 hour (+ refrigeration) **makes** 6
nutritional count per pie 22.1g total fat (13.9g saturated fat); 1946kJ (464 cal); 57.1g carbohydrate; 7.2g protein; 3.9g fibre
tips You need 4 large stems of rhubarb this recipe.
If pastry is too dry, add 2 teaspoons of water with the egg yolk.

apple, date and orange pie

8 medium granny smith apples (1.2kg), peeled, cored, sliced thickly
½ cup (125ml) water
1½ cups (210g) coarsely chopped seeded dried dates
¼ cup (55g) caster sugar
2 teaspoons finely grated orange rind
1 tablespoon demerara sugar
pastry
1 cup (150g) plain flour
½ cup (75g) self-raising flour
¼ cup (35g) cornflour
¼ cup (30g) custard powder
1 tablespoon caster sugar
100g cold butter, chopped coarsely
1 egg, separated
¼ cup (60ml) iced water, approximately

1 Make pastry.
2 Meanwhile, combine apple and the water in large saucepan; bring to the boil. Reduce heat; simmer, covered, about 5 minutes. Add dates; cook further 5 minutes or until apples soften. Drain well; transfer apple mixture to medium bowl, stir in caster sugar and rind. Cool.
3 Preheat oven to 220°C/200°C fan-forced. Grease deep 25cm pie dish.
4 Roll two-thirds of the pastry between sheets of baking paper until large enough to line dish. Lift pastry into dish; trim edge. Spoon apple mixture into dish; brush edge with egg white.
5 Roll out remaining pastry large enough to cover pie. Place pastry over filling; press edge together to seal. Brush pastry with egg white; sprinkle with demerara sugar.
6 Bake 20 minutes. Reduce oven to 180°C/160°C fan-forced; bake further 25 minutes.
pastry Process flours, custard powder, sugar and butter until crumbly. Add egg yolk and enough of the water to process until ingredients come together. Knead dough on floured surface until smooth. Enclose in plastic wrap; refrigerate 30 minutes.

prep + cook time 1 hour (+ refrigeration) **serves** 8
nutritional count per serving 14.2g total fat (8.7g saturated fat); 1818kJ (435 cal); 69.2g carbohydrate; 6.3g protein; 6.2g fibre

apricot and almond apple pie

10 medium granny smith apples
(1.5kg), peeled, cored,
sliced thickly
½ cup (125ml) water
1 tablespoon caster sugar
⅔ cup (220g) apricot jam
1 teaspoon finely grated
lemon rind
¼ cup (20g) flaked almonds

pastry
1 cup (150g) plain flour
½ cup (75g) self-raising flour
¼ cup (35g) cornflour
¼ cup (30g) custard powder
1 tablespoon caster sugar
100g cold butter,
chopped coarsely
1 egg, separated
¼ cup (60ml) iced water,
approximately

1 Make pastry.

2 Meanwhile, combine apple and the water in large saucepan; bring
to the boil. Reduce heat; simmer, covered, about 10 minutes or until
apples soften. Drain well; transfer apples to medium bowl, stir in sugar,
jam and rind. Cool.

3 Preheat oven to 220°C/200°C fan-forced. Grease deep 25cm pie dish.

4 Roll two-third of the pastry between sheets of baking paper until large
enough to line dish. Lift pastry into dish; trim edge. Spoon apple mixture
into dish; brush edge with egg white.

5 Roll out remaining pastry large enough to cover pie. Place pastry
over filling; press edge together to seal. Brush pastry with egg white;
sprinkle with nuts.

6 Bake pie 20 minutes. Reduce oven to 180°C/160°C fan-forced;
bake further 25 minutes.

pastry Process flours, custard powder, sugar and butter until crumbly.
Add egg yolk and enough of the water to process until ingredients come
together. Knead dough on floured surface until smooth. Enclose in plastic
wrap; refrigerate 30 minutes.

prep + cook time 1 hour (+ refrigeration) **serves** 8
nutritional count per serving 15.5g total fat (8.8g saturated fat);
1814kJ (434 cal); 66.6g carbohydrate; 6.5g protein; 4.7g fibre

lemon meringue pie

½ cup (75g) cornflour
1 cup (220g) caster sugar
½ cup (125ml) lemon juice
1¼ cups (310ml) water
2 teaspoons finely grated
   lemon rind
60g unsalted butter, chopped
3 eggs, separated
½ cup (110g) caster sugar, extra

pastry
1½ cups (225g) plain flour
1 tablespoon icing sugar
140g cold butter, chopped
1 egg yolk
2 tablespoons cold water

1 Make pastry.
2 Grease 24cm-round loose-based fluted flan tin. Roll pastry between sheets of baking paper until large enough to line tin. Ease pastry into tin, press into base and side; trim edge. Cover; refrigerate 30 minutes.
3 Preheat oven to 240°C/220°C fan-forced.
4 Place tin on oven tray. Line pastry case with baking paper; fill with dried beans or rice. Bake 15 minutes; remove paper and beans. Bake further 10 minutes; cool pie shell, turn oven off.
5 Meanwhile, combine cornflour and sugar in medium saucepan; gradually stir in juice and the water until smooth. Cook, stirring, over high heat, until mixture boils and thickens. Reduce heat; simmer, stirring, 1 minute. Remove from heat; stir in rind, butter and egg yolks. Cool 10 minutes.
6 Spread filling into pie shell. Cover; refrigerate 2 hours.
7 Preheat oven to 240°C/220°C fan-forced.
8 Beat egg whites in small bowl with electric mixer until soft peaks form; gradually add extra sugar, beating until sugar dissolves.
9 Roughen surface of filling with fork before spreading with meringue mixture. Bake about 2 minutes or until browned lightly.
pastry Process flour, icing sugar and butter until crumbly. Add egg yolk and the water; process until ingredients come together. Knead dough on floured surface until smooth. Cover; refrigerate 30 minutes.

prep + cook time 1 hour (+ refrigeration) **serves** 10
nutritional count per serving 19g total fat (11.5g saturated fat); 1739kJ (416 cal); 57.1g carbohydrate; 5.2g protein; 0.9g fibre

black bottom pie

90g butter
¼ cup (55g) caster sugar
1 egg
1 cup (150g) plain flour
¼ cup (35g) self-raising flour
½ cup (125ml) thickened cream
30g dark eating chocolate, grated

filling
1 tablespoon gelatine
¼ cup (60ml) milk
¼ cup (55g) caster sugar
3 teaspoons cornflour
1 cup (250ml) milk, extra
3 eggs, separated
60g dark eating chocolate, melted
1 teaspoon vanilla extract
¼ cup (55g) caster sugar, extra

1 Beat butter and sugar in small bowl with electric mixer until just combined. Beat in egg. Stir in sifted flours, in two batches. Turn dough onto floured surface; knead until smooth. Cover; refrigerate 30 minutes.
2 Meanwhile, make filling.
3 Preheat oven to 200°C/180°C fan-forced. Roll pastry on floured surface until large enough to line 23cm pie plate. Ease pastry into plate, press into base and side; trim edge. Prick pastry all over with fork.
4 Bake pastry case 15 minutes or until browned; cool.
5 Spread chocolate custard into pastry case; refrigerate until firm. Spread vanilla custard into pastry case; refrigerate until firm. Spread whipped cream over custard, then sprinkle with extra chocolate.
filling Sprinkle gelatine over milk in small jug. Blend sugar and cornflour with extra milk in small saucepan; stir over heat until mixture boils and thickens, remove from heat. Quickly stir in egg yolks, then gelatine mixture; stir until smooth. Divide custard into two bowls. Stir chocolate into one bowl. Cover both bowls; cool to room temperature. Stir extract into plain custard. Beat egg whites in small bowl with electric mixer until soft peaks form; gradually add extra sugar, beating until dissolved after additions. Fold egg white mixture into vanilla custard, in two batches.

prep + cook time 1 hour (+ refrigeration) **serves** 8
nutritional count per serving 23g total fat (13.8g saturated fat); 1806kJ (432 cal); 47.6g carbohydrate; 9.9g protein; 1g fibre

apple and marmalade freeform pie

2½ cups (375g) plain flour
185g cold butter, chopped
2 egg yolks
½ cup (60g) finely grated cheddar cheese
¼ cup (60ml) water, approximately
6 medium apples (900g)
2 tablespoons water, extra
2 tablespoons brown sugar
2 teaspoons milk
¼ cup (85g) citrus marmalade

1 Process flour and butter until crumbly; add egg yolks, cheese and enough water to form a soft dough. Knead dough on floured surface until smooth. Cover; refrigerate 30 minutes.
2 Preheat oven to 200°C/180°C fan-forced.
3 Peel, core and halve apples; cut each half into six wedges. Cook apple with the extra water and sugar in medium saucepan, covered, stirring occasionally, about 5 minutes or until apple has just softened. Cool to room temperature.
4 Roll pastry between two sheets of baking paper to form 40cm circle. Remove top sheet of paper, turn pastry onto oven tray. Remove remaining sheet of baking paper.
5 Spread apple mixture over pastry, leaving a 5cm border. Dollop teaspoons of the marmalade onto apple mixture. Fold pastry up to partly enclose fruit; brush pastry evenly with milk.
6 Bake pie about 30 minutes or until pastry is cooked and browned lightly. Dust with icing sugar, if you like, before serving.

prep + cook time 1 hour (+ refrigeration) **serves** 6
nutritional count per serving 31.3g total fat (19.5g saturated fat); 3687kJ (882 cal); 140g carbohydrate; 11.2g protein; 5.7g fibre

peanut butter and fudge ice-cream pie

300g packet chocolate chip cookies
40g butter, melted
1 tablespoon milk
1 litre vanilla ice-cream, softened
1⅓ cups (375g) crunchy peanut butter
hot fudge sauce
200g dark chocolate, chopped coarsely
50g white marshmallows, chopped coarsely
300ml thickened cream

1 Grease 24cm-round loose-based flan tin.
2 Blend or process cookies until mixture resembles coarse breadcrumbs.
Add butter and milk; process until combined.
3 Press cookie mixture evenly over base and around side of tin;
refrigerate 10 minutes.
4 Beat softened ice-cream and peanut butter in large bowl with
electric mixer until combined. Spoon pie filling into crumb crust.
Cover; freeze pie 3 hours or overnight.
5 Make hot fudge sauce.
6 Serve pie, drizzled with fudge sauce.
hot fudge sauce Stir ingredients in small saucepan over heat,
without boiling, until smooth.

prep + cook time 30 minutes (+ freezing) **serves** 10
nutritional count per serving 49.2g total fat (21.4g saturated fat);
2922kJ (699 cal); 49.4g carbohydrate; 16g protein; 5g fibre
tips Use a good quality ice-cream; various ice-creams differ from
manufacturer to manufacturer, depending on the quantities of air and
fat incorporated into the mixture. Marshmallows come in a variety of
sizes and colours; the largest white type is best for this recipe.

apple cranberry turnovers

40g butter
4 medium apples (600g), peeled, chopped finely
¼ cup (55g) firmly packed brown sugar
⅓ cup (45g) dried cranberries
⅓ cup (35g) coarsely chopped roasted walnuts
1 teaspoon ground cinnamon
2 teaspoons lemon juice
12 sheets fillo pastry
75g butter, melted

1 Melt butter in large frying pan; cook apple, stirring, about 10 minutes or until apple is tender. Add sugar; stir until dissolved. Remove from heat, stir in cranberries, nuts, cinnamon and juice. Cool.
2 Preheat oven to 220°C/200°C fan-forced. Grease oven trays.
3 Place four sheets of pastry on top of each other; cover remaining sheets with baking paper then a damp tea towel. Cut six 12cm rounds from pastry. Brush between each layer of pastry with some of the melted butter. Repeat with remaining sheets (you will have 18 pastry rounds).
4 Divide apple mixture among pastry rounds. Fold over pastry to enclose filling, pressing edges together. Brush turnovers with remaining butter.
5 Bake turnovers about 8 minutes or until browned lightly. Serve turnovers immediately with ice-cream, if you like.

prep + cook time 45 minutes **makes** 18
nutritional count per turnover 6.8g total fat (3.6g saturated fat); 497kJ (119 cal); 12.7g carbohydrate; 1.4g protein; 0.9g fibre

spiced stone fruit strudel

2 medium peaches (300g), quartered, sliced thinly
2 medium nectarines (340g), quartered, sliced thinly
2 tablespoons brown sugar
½ cup (80g) sultanas
1 ½ teaspoons ground cinnamon
½ teaspoon ground nutmeg
⅓ cup (25g) fresh breadcrumbs
6 sheets fillo pastry
20g butter, melted
2 tablespoons milk
2 teaspoons icing sugar

1 Combine peach, nectarine, brown sugar, sultanas, spices and breadcrumbs in medium bowl.
2 Preheat oven to 200°C/180°C fan-forced. Grease oven tray; line with baking paper.
3 Stack fillo sheets, brushing all sheets with half of the combined butter and milk. Cut fillo stack in half widthways; cover one stack with baking paper, then with a damp tea towel, to prevent drying out.
4 Place half of the fruit mixture along centre of uncovered fillo stack; roll from one side to enclose filling, sealing ends of roll with a little of the remaining butter mixture. Place strudel, seam-side down, on tray; brush all over with a little of the remaining butter mixture. Repeat process with remaining fillo stack, fruit mixture and butter mixture.
5 Bake strudels about 25 minutes or until browned. Cut each strudel in half widthways; divide among plates, dust with sifted icing sugar.

prep + cook time 45 minutes **serves** 4
nutritional count per serving 5.5g total fat (3.1g saturated fat); 1191kJ (285 cal); 53.1g carbohydrate; 5.9g protein; 4.2g fibre

pumpkin pie

1 cup (150g) plain flour
¼ cup (35g) self-raising flour
2 tablespoons cornflour
2 tablespoons icing sugar
125g butter, chopped
2 tablespoons water, approximately
filling
2 eggs
¼ cup (55g) brown sugar
2 tablespoons maple syrup
1 cup cooked mashed pumpkin
⅔ cup (160ml) evaporated milk
1 teaspoon ground cinnamon
½ teaspoon ground nutmeg
pinch ground allspice

1 Sift flours and sugar into bowl; rub in butter. Add enough water to make ingredients cling together. Press dough into a ball, knead gently on floured surface until smooth; cover, refrigerate 30 minutes.
2 Preheat oven to 200°C/180°C fan-forced.
3 Roll dough on floured surface until large enough to line 23cm pie plate. Lift pastry into pie plate, ease into side; trim edge. Use scraps of pastry to make a double edge of pastry; trim and decorate edge.
4 Place pie plate on oven tray; line pastry with paper, fill with dried beans or rice. Bake 10 minutes. Remove paper and beans; bake further 10 minutes or until lightly browned, cool.
5 Meanwhile, make filling.
6 Reduce oven to 180°C/160°C fan-forced.
7 Pour filling into pastry case; bake about 50 minutes or until filling is set. Cool. Serve dusted with extra sifted icing sugar, if you like.
filling Beat eggs, sugar and maple syrup in small bowl with electric mixer until thick. Stir in pumpkin, milk and spices.

prep + cook time 1 hour 15 minutes (+ refrigeration) **serves** 8
nutritional count per serving 15.9g total fat (9.8g saturated fat); 1333kJ (319 cal); 37.4g carbohydrate; 6.8g protein; 1.3g fibre
tip You will need to cook about 350g pumpkin for this recipe.

SAVOURY TARTS
& TARTLETS

spinach and pumpkin fillo pie

75g butter, melted
1 tablespoon olive oil
1 medium brown onion (150g), chopped finely
2 cloves garlic, crushed
1kg butternut pumpkin, chopped finely
1 tablespoon brown sugar
1 teaspoon ground cumin
½ teaspoon ground nutmeg
2 x 250g frozen spinach, thawed, drained
1 cup (200g) fetta cheese
2 eggs, beaten lightly
6 sheets fillo pastry

1 Brush 24cm ovenproof pie dish with some of the butter.
2 Heat oil in large frying pan; cook onion and garlic, stirring, until onion softens. Add pumpkin, sugar and spices; cook, covered, 20 minutes or until pumpkin is tender. Stir in spinach and ¾ cup of the cheese. Remove from heat; cool 5 minutes. Stir in egg.
3 Preheat oven to 180°C/160°C fan-forced.
4 Layer two sheets of pastry, brushing each with butter; fold pastry in half widthways, place in pie dish, edges overhanging. Brush pastry with butter again. Repeat with remaining pastry, overlapping the pieces clockwise around the dish. Fold over edges to make a rim around the edge of the pie; brush with remaining butter. Spoon pumpkin mixture into dish.
5 Bake pie about 40 minutes or until browned lightly. Sprinkle with remaining cheese.

prep + cook time 1 hour **serves** 6
nutritional count per serving 24.4g total fat (13.4g saturated fat); 1588kJ (380 cal); 23.2g carbohydrate; 15g protein; 5.1g fibre

sun-dried tomato and zucchini quiche

½ cup (100g) cottage cheese
100g butter, softened
1⅓ cups (200g) plain flour
1 tablespoon olive oil
1 medium brown onion (150g), sliced thinly
¼ cup (35g) drained, finely chopped sun-dried tomatoes
⅓ cup (70g) drained sun-dried zucchini
¼ cup finely shredded fresh basil leaves
¾ cup (60g) grated gruyère cheese
¼ cup (20g) grated parmesan cheese
3 eggs
¾ cup (180ml) cream
¼ cup (30g) grated tasty cheese

1 Combine cottage cheese and butter in large bowl; stir in flour.
Press dough into ball; knead gently on floured surface until smooth.
Cover; refrigerate 30 minutes.
2 Preheat oven to 200°C/180°C fan-forced.
3 Roll dough on floured surface until large enough to line 24cm-round
flan tin. Ease pastry into tin; trim edge. Place tin on oven tray. Line pastry
with paper; fill with dried beans or rice. Bake 10 minutes. Remove paper
and beans; bake further 10 minutes or until browned.
4 Reduce oven to 180°C/160°C fan-forced.
5 Heat oil in medium saucepan; cook onion, stirring, until soft. Drain on
absorbent paper.
6 Spread onion, tomato, zucchini, basil, gruyère and parmesan into pastry
case. Top with combined eggs and cream; sprinkle with tasty cheese.
Bake quiche about 35 minutes or until set.

prep + cook time 1 hour (+ refrigeration) **serves** 6
nutritional count per serving 40.6g total fat (23.5g saturated fat);
2299kJ (550 cal); 29g carbohydrate; 16.9g protein; 2.7g fibre

spinach, chickpea and fetta tart

500g coarsely chopped frozen spinach, thawed
1 tablespoon olive oil
1 medium brown onion (150g), chopped finely
3 cloves garlic, crushed
420g can chickpeas, drained, rinsed
400g fresh ricotta cheese
4 eggs, beaten lightly
½ cup (40g) finely grated parmesan cheese
¼ cup finely chopped fresh dill
6 sheets fillo pastry
50g butter, melted
100g fetta cheese, crumbled

1 Squeeze the excess moisture from the spinach; spread out on absorbent paper.
2 Heat oil in small frying pan; cook onion and garlic over medium heat, stirring, until onion is tender. Cool. Combine onion mixture, spinach, chickpeas, ricotta, eggs, parmesan and dill in large bowl; mix well.
3 Preheat oven to 200°C/180°C fan-forced. Grease 22cm springform tin.
4 Brush each sheet of fillo with melted butter; fold each in half to enclose buttered side and form square shape. Gently press sheets, overlapping, into base and sides of tin to line. Spread spinach mixture into tin; gently push down fillo around sides of tin to neaten. Sprinkle with fetta. Place tin on oven tray.
5 Bake tart about 40 minutes or until just set. Cool in pan.

prep + cook time 1 hour **serves** 8
nutritional count per serving 21.9g total fat (11.3g saturated fat); 1413kJ (338 cal); 14.1g carbohydrate; 19.2g protein; 5.4g fibre

mushroom and bacon brunch tarts

4 rindless bacon rashers (260g), chopped
125g butter
200g swiss brown mushrooms, halved
2 teaspoons worcestershire sauce
8 sheets fillo pastry
12 small eggs (50g each)
2 tablespoons finely chopped fresh chives

1 Preheat oven to 200°C/180°C fan-forced. Grease 12-hole (⅓-cup/80ml) muffin pan.
2 Cook bacon in heated frying pan until just cooked; drain.
3 Heat 30g of the butter in same pan; cook mushrooms, stirring, until browned. Stir in sauce.
4 Melt remaining butter. Brush one pastry sheet with butter, top with another sheet. Repeat with two more sheets of pastry. Cut through the four layers of pastry into 10cm squares. Place one square diagonally over another to give eight points. Press pastry into one pan hole. Repeat with remaining pastry sheets and butter.
5 Break eggs into pastry cases, top with mushroom mixture and bacon.
6 Bake tarts 20 minutes or until pastry is browned. Just before serving, sprinkle tarts with chives and freshly ground black pepper.

prep + cook time 45 minutes **makes** 12
nutritional count per tart 15.9g total fat (8g saturated fat); 903kJ (216 cal); 7g carbohydrate; 11.3g protein; 0.7g fibre

onion and anchovy tartlets

1 tablespoon olive oil
60g butter
3 medium brown onions (450g), halved, sliced thinly
2 cloves garlic, crushed
1 bay leaf
3 sprigs fresh thyme
⅓ cup coarsely chopped fresh flat-leaf parsley
8 anchovy fillets, drained, chopped finely
2 tablespoons coarsely chopped seeded black olives
¾ cup (110g) self-raising flour
¾ cup (110g) plain flour
¾ cup (180ml) buttermilk

1 Heat oil and half of the butter in large frying pan; cook onion, garlic, bay leaf and thyme, stirring occasionally, about 20 minutes or until onion caramelises. Discard bay leaf and thyme; stir in parsley, anchovy and olives.
2 Meanwhile, blend or process flours and remaining butter until fine. Add buttermilk; process until ingredients come together. Knead dough on floured surface until smooth.
3 Preheat oven to 220°C/200°C fan-forced. Grease two oven trays.
4 Divide dough into six pieces; roll each piece of dough on floured surface into 14cm squares. Fold edges over to form 1cm border. Place squares on trays; place rounded tablespoons of the onion mixture on each square.
5 Bake tartlets about 15 minutes.

prep + cook time 1 hour **makes** 6
nutritional count per tartlet 12.9g total fat (6.4g saturated fat); 1191kJ (285 cal); 33.1g carbohydrate; 7.7g protein; 2.7g fibre

tomato tarte tatins
with crème fraîche sauce

9 small firm tomatoes (800g),
  peeled, quartered
30g butter
1 clove garlic, crushed
1 tablespoon brown sugar
2 tablespoons balsamic vinegar
1½ sheets butter puff pastry,
  thawed
1 egg
vegetable oil, for deep-frying
6 sprigs fresh baby basil

crème fraîche sauce
20g butter
2 shallots (50g), chopped finely
1 cup (240g) crème fraîche
⅓ cup (80ml) water

1 Preheat oven to 220°C/200°C fan-forced.
2 Discard pulp and seeds from tomato quarters; gently flatten flesh.
3 Melt butter in large frying pan; cook garlic, stirring, over low heat, until fragrant. Add sugar and vinegar; cook, stirring, until sugar dissolves. Place tomato in pan, in single layer; cook, covered, turning once, about 5 minutes or until tomato softens.
4 Grease six 1 cup (250ml) metal pie dishes; cut six 11cm rounds from pastry sheets. Divide tomato among dishes; top each with one pastry round, pressing down gently. Brush pastry with egg; bake about 15 minutes or until pastry is browned lightly.
5 Meanwhile, heat oil in small saucepan; place thoroughly dry basil sprigs, one at a time, in pan. Deep-fry about 3 seconds or until basil is crisp. Drain on absorbent paper.
6 Make crème fraîche sauce.
7 Divide sauce among serving plates; turn tarts onto sauce, top with basil.
crème fraîche sauce Melt butter in small saucepan; cook shallot, stirring, about 3 minutes or until softened. Add crème fraîche; cook, stirring, over low heat, until heated through. Stir in the water.

prep + cook time 1 hour **serves** 6
nutritional count per serving 33.7g total fat (20.4g saturated fat); 1735kJ (415 cal); 21.2g carbohydrate; 6.1g protein; 2.4g fibre

caramelised onion and beetroot tart

50g butter
4 medium red onions (680g),
  halved, sliced thinly
1 tablespoon red wine vinegar
1 teaspoon fresh thyme leaves
3 medium beetroot (500g),
  trimmed
1 sheet butter puff pastry, thawed
cooking-oil spray
120g baby rocket leaves

chive oil
½ cup coarsely chopped
  fresh chives
¾ cup (180ml) olive oil
1 ice cube

horseradish cream
¾ cup (180ml) cream
1 tablespoon horseradish cream

1 Melt butter in medium frying pan; cook onion, stirring occasionally, over medium heat about 30 minutes or until caramelised. Stir in vinegar and thyme.

2 Meanwhile, boil or steam unpeeled beetroot until tender; drain. When cool enough to handle, peel beetroot; slice thinly.

3 Preheat oven to 220°C/200°C fan-forced. Grease oven tray.

4 Place pastry sheet on flat surface; cut a 24cm circle out of pastry. Place on tray, prick all over with fork; freeze 10 minutes.

5 Bake pastry about 5 minutes or until browned lightly.

6 Make chive oil. Make horseradish cream.

7 Spread onion mixture over pastry; top with slightly overlapping beetroot slices. Spray tart lightly with oil; bake about 10 minutes.

8 Meanwhile, combine rocket in medium bowl with half of the chive oil; divide among serving plates.

9 Cut tart into six wedges. Place each wedge on rocket, drizzle with remaining chive oil; serve with horseradish cream.

chive oil Blend or process ingredients until smooth.

horseradish cream Beat cream in small bowl with electric mixer until soft peaks form; fold in horseradish cream.

prep + cook time 1 hour (+ freezing) **serves** 6
nutritional count per serving 54.5g total fat (20.6g saturated fat); 2554kJ (611 cal); 24.2g carbohydrate; 5.8g protein; 4.6g fibre

leek quiche

45g butter
4 sheets fillo pastry
4 small leeks (800g)
45g butter, extra
1 clove garlic, crushed
125g fetta cheese
⅔ cup (160ml) cream
3 eggs, beaten lightly

1 Preheat oven to 180°C/160°C fan-forced.
2 Melt butter; brush each layer of pastry with melted butter, fold each layer over in half. Layer pastry, one folded piece on top of the other to give eight layers. Place pie plate (base measurement 18cm) upside down on layered pastry; using plate as a guide, cut around plate making circle 1cm larger than the plate. Carefully lift all layers of pastry into plate, leave pastry standing up around edge of plate.
3 Trim ends of leeks, leave about 5cm of the green tops; slice leeks finely, wash well under cold running water, drain well.
4 Melt extra butter in pan; cook leek and garlic, stirring, about 5 minutes over low heat until leeks are just tender. Stir in sieved cheese, cream and eggs; season with ground black pepper. Pour mixture into pastry case.
5 Bake quiche about 45 minutes or until golden brown.

prep + cook time 1 hour 15 minutes **serves** 6
nutritional count per serving 32.2g total fat (19.9g saturated fat); 1572kJ (376 cal); 10.4g carbohydrate; 10.9g protein; 2.7g fibre

tomato and basil quiche

1 cup (150g) plain flour
75g butter, chopped
1 egg yolk
1 tablespoon lemon juice, approximately
30g butter, extra
1 medium leek (350g), sliced thinly
3 eggs
300ml cream
¾ cup (90g) grated cheddar cheese
3 small ripe tomatoes (270g), peeled, cut into 1cm slices
¾ cup coarsely chopped fresh basil
½ cup coarsely chopped flat-leaf parsley
1 tablespoon finely grated parmesan cheese

1 Sift flour into bowl, rub in chopped butter. Add egg yolk and enough juice to mix to firm dough. Cover; refrigerate 30 minutes.
2 Preheat oven to 200°C/180°C fan-forced. Grease 23cm flan tin.
3 Roll pastry on floured surface until large enough to line flan tin. Ease pastry into tin, press into base and side; trim edge. Line tin with baking paper; fill with dry beans or rice. Bake about 10 minutes. Remove paper and beans; bake further 5 minutes.
4 Meanwhile, melt extra butter in medium frying pan; cook leek, stirring, until tender. Combine eggs, cream and cheese in medium bowl, stir in leek mixture; pour into pastry case. Roll edge of tomato slices in combined basil and parsley, place on top of leek mixture; sprinkle with cheese. Bake quiche about 30 minutes.

prep + cook time 45 minutes (+ refrigeration) **serves** 8
nutritional count per serving 47.7g total fat (29.8g saturated fat); 2391kJ (572 cal); 22.1g carbohydrate; 13.6g protein; 2.9g fibre

egg and cheese tartlets with capsicum relish

2 sheets puff pastry
2 teaspoons olive oil
2 shallots (50g), sliced thinly
4 eggs
¼ cup (60ml) cream
½ cup (40g) finely grated
    parmesan cheese
30g baby rocket leaves

capsicum relish
1 tablespoon olive oil
1 small red onion (100g),
    sliced thinly
2 medium red capsicum (400g),
    sliced thinly
⅓ cup (80ml) white balsamic
    vinegar
2 tablespoons brown sugar
½ cup (125ml) water

1 Preheat oven to 220°C/200°C fan-forced. Oil a six-hole (¾-cup/180ml) texas muffin pan.

2 Cut pastry sheets in half; cut halves into three rectangles. Overlap two rectangles to form cross shapes; push gently into pan holes to cover bases and sides. Prick bases with fork. Line each pastry case with baking paper; fill with dried beans or rice. Bake 10 minutes. Remove paper and beans; bake about 5 minutes or until browned lightly. Cool cases in pan. Reduce oven to 200°C/180°C fan-forced.

3 Meanwhile, make capsicum relish.

4 Heat oil in small frying pan; cook shallots, stirring, until soft.

5 Whisk eggs and cream in medium bowl; mix in cheese and shallots. Spoon egg mixture into pastry cases.

6 Bake tartlets about 15 minutes or until set. Serve with relish and rocket.

capsicum relish Heat oil in large frying pan; cook onion and capsicum about 10 minutes or until vegetables are soft. Add vinegar, sugar and the water; cook, stirring occasionally, about 15 minutes or until mixture thickens slightly.

prep + cook time 1 hour (+ cooling) **serves** 6
nutritional count per serving 27.3g total fat (12.7g saturated fat); 1697kJ (406 cal); 28g carbohydrate; 11.7g protein; 1.7g fibre
tip Balsamic white vinegar is a clear and lighter version of balsamic vinegar; it has a fresh, sweet clean taste, and is available from major supermarkets and delicatessens.

169

gruyère, leek and bacon tart

50g butter
2 medium leeks (700g), sliced thinly
2 rindless bacon rashers (130g), chopped finely
2 sheets puff pastry
2 eggs
½ cup (125ml) cream
1 teaspoon fresh thyme leaves
½ cup (60g) finely grated gruyère cheese

1 Preheat oven to 220°C/200°C fan-forced. Oil 24cm-round loose-based flan tin; place tin on oven tray.
2 Melt butter in medium frying pan; cook leek, stirring occasionally, about 15 minutes or until soft. Remove from pan. Cook bacon in same pan, stirring, until crisp; drain on absorbent paper.
3 Meanwhile, place one pastry sheet in flan tin; overlap with second sheet to form cross shape, trim away overlapping pastry. Prick pastry base with fork, line with baking paper; fill with dried beans or rice. Bake 20 minutes. Remove paper and beans; cool pastry case. Reduce oven to 200°C/180°C fan-forced.
4 Whisk eggs, cream and thyme in small bowl.
5 Spread leek into pastry case; top with bacon. Pour in egg mixture; sprinkle with cheese.
6 Bake tart about 20 minutes or until filling sets. Cool 10 minutes before serving. Serve with a baby rocket and parmesan salad, if you like.

prep + cook time 1 hour **serves** 8
nutritional count per serving 27.2g total fat (11.1g saturated fat); 1505kJ (360 cal); 17.6g carbohydrate; 10.8g protein; 2.1g fibre

tomato, leek and marinated fetta tartlets

1 medium leek (350g)
20g butter
1 tablespoon olive oil
2 sheets puff pastry
250g cherry tomatoes,
  sliced thinly
½ teaspoon fresh thyme leaves
1 tablespoon red wine vinegar

marinated fetta
1 teaspoon finely grated lemon rind
¼ teaspoon cracked black pepper
2 cloves garlic, crushed
2 teaspoons fresh thyme leaves
200g fetta cheese,
  cut into 24 pieces
1¼ cups (310ml) olive oil

1 Make marinated fetta.

2 Preheat oven to 220°C/200°C fan-forced. Oil oven trays.

3 Cut leek into 6cm pieces; cut pieces in half lengthways, slice halves lengthways into thin strips. Heat butter and oil in large frying pan; cook leek, stirring occasionally, about 20 minutes or until soft.

4 Meanwhile, cut each pastry sheet into twelve 6cm x 8cm rectangles; place on trays. Fold in each side to form a 2mm border; prick pastry pieces with fork. Bake, uncovered, about 10 minutes or until browned lightly. Remove from oven; using fork, immediately press pastry pieces down to flatten. Reduce oven to 200°C/180°C fan-forced.

5 Meanwhile, place tomato in medium bowl with thyme and vinegar; toss gently to combine.

6 Spread 1 tablespoon of the leek mixture over each pastry piece; crumble one piece of the cheese over each then top with tomato mixture. Bake about 5 minutes or until tomato just softens. Serve immediately.

marinated fetta Combine rind, pepper, garlic and thyme in medium sterilised glass jar with a tight-fitting lid; add cheese. Seal jar then shake gently to coat cheese in mixture. Open jar and pour in enough of the oil to completely cover cheese mixture. Reseal; refrigerate overnight.

prep + cook time 1 hour (+ refrigeration) **makes** 24
nutritional count per tartlet 7.2g total fat (2.2g saturated fat);
414kJ (99 cal); 5.6g carbohydrate; 2.5g protein; 0.7g fibre
tip Work with one puff pastry sheet at a time, keeping the other in the freezer so that it doesn't become too soft.

goats cheese and roast vegie tart

1 sheet butter puff pastry
2 cloves garlic, crushed
2 tablespoons fresh oregano leaves
3 cups (500g) coarsely chopped roasted vegetables
1 medium egg tomato (75g), chopped coarsely
150g goats cheese, crumbled
1 tablespoon fresh oregano leaves, extra

1 Preheat oven to 240°C/220°C fan-forced. Line oven tray with baking paper.
2 Place pastry sheet on tray; spread with garlic and sprinkle with oregano. Top with vegetables, tomato and cheese.
3 Bake tart about 20 minutes or until pastry is browned lightly; sprinkle with extra oregano.

prep + cook time 30 minutes **serves** 4
nutritional count per serving 18.1g total fat (9.6g saturated fat); 1304kJ (312 cal); 24.3g carbohydrate; 10.9g protein; 4.7g fibre

quiche lorraine

1 medium brown onion (150g), chopped finely
3 rindless bacon rashers (195g), chopped finely
3 eggs
300ml cream
½ cup (125ml) milk
¾ cup (120g) coarsely grated gruyère cheese
pastry
1¾ cups (260g) plain flour
150g cold butter, chopped coarsely
1 egg yolk
2 teaspoons lemon juice
⅓ cup (80ml) iced water, approximately

1 Make pastry.
2 Preheat oven to 200°C/180°C fan-forced.
3 Roll pastry between sheets of baking paper large enough to line a deep 23cm loose-based flan tin. Lift pastry into tin; gently press pastry around side. Trim edge, place tin on oven tray. Cover pastry with baking paper; fill with dried beans or rice. Bake 10 minutes; remove paper and beans. Bake pastry a further 10 minutes or until golden brown; cool.
4 Reduce oven temperature to 180°C/160°C fan-forced.
5 Cook onion and bacon in heated oiled small frying pan until onion is soft; drain on absorbent paper, cool. Sprinkle bacon mixture over pastry case.
6 Whisk eggs in medium bowl then whisk in cream, milk and cheese; pour into pastry case. Bake about 35 minutes or until filling is set. Stand 5 minutes before removing quiche from tin.
pastry Sift flour into bowl; rub in butter. Add egg yolk, juice and enough water to make ingredients cling together. Knead gently on floured surface until smooth. Cover; refrigerate 30 minutes.

prep + cook time 1 hour 30 minutes (+ refrigeration) **serves** 6
nutritional count per serving 51.8g total fat (35.4g saturated fat); 3139kJ (751 cal); 35.4g carbohydrate; 22.1g protein; 2g fibre

moroccan tart

1 sheet shortcrust pastry, thawed
1 tablespoon olive oil
300g lamb mince
1 teaspoon ground coriander
½ teaspoon ground cinnamon
400g can chickpeas, rinsed, drained
1 clove garlic, crushed
2 tablespoons lemon juice
1 piece preserved lemon (35g), trimmed, chopped finely
2 tablespoons roasted pine nuts
125g fetta cheese, crumbled

1 Preheat oven to 200°C/180°C fan-forced. Oil oven tray.
2 Roll pastry out to 28cm x 30cm rectangle; place on tray. Fold edges of pastry over to make a 1cm border all the way around pastry. Prick pastry base with fork; bake 10 minutes.
3 Meanwhile, heat half of the oil in medium frying pan; cook lamb, coriander and cinnamon, stirring, 5 minutes. Drain away excess oil.
4 Combine chickpeas, garlic, juice and remaining oil in medium bowl. Using fork, coarsely mash mixture; stir in preserved lemon. Spread over pastry base. Top with lamb mixture; sprinkle with nuts and cheese.
5 Bake tart about 10 minutes.

prep + cook time 45 minutes **serves** 4
nutritional count per serving 34.8g total fat (14.3g saturated fat); 2274kJ (544 cal); 27.7g carbohydrate; 28.4g protein; 4.4g fibre

caramelised onion and ricotta tarts

40g butter
1 tablespoon olive oil
3 large brown onions (600g), sliced thinly
2 tablespoons brown sugar
2 tablespoons balsamic vinegar
½ cup (125ml) water
2 sheets puff pastry
¼ cup (60g) ricotta cheese

1 Oil four 12cm loose-based flan tins.
2 Melt butter with oil in large frying pan; cook onion, sugar and vinegar, stirring, until very soft and browned lightly. Add the water; cook, stirring, until water has evaporated.
3 Meanwhile, cut pastry sheets in half diagonally. Line tins with pastry, press into sides; trim edges, prick bases with fork. Freeze 15 minutes.
4 Preheat oven to 220°C/200°C fan-forced.
5 Place tins on oven tray; bake 15 minutes.
6 Top tarts with caramelised onion, gently push onion down to flatten pastry; sprinkle with cheese. Bake about 5 minutes.

prep + cook time 45 minutes (+ freezing) **makes** 4
nutritional count per tart 33.5g total fat (17.3g saturated fat); 2161kJ (517 cal); 44.6g carbohydrate; 8.4g protein; 3.1g fibre

tomato, pesto and olive tart

500g grape tomatoes
1 tablespoon balsamic vinegar
1 tablespoon olive oil
1 sheet puff pasty
2 tablespoons basil pesto
⅓ cup (55g) seeded black olives
1½ cups (360g) ricotta cheese

1 Preheat oven to 220°C/200°C fan-forced.
2 Combine tomatoes in medium bowl with vinegar and half the oil; spread tomatoes on oven tray. Roast, uncovered, about 10 minutes or until tomatoes collapse.
3 Place pastry on oiled oven tray. Fold edges of pastry over to make a 5mm border all the way around pastry; prick base with fork. Place another oven tray on top of pastry; bake 10 minutes. Remove top tray from pastry. Reduce oven to 200°C/180°C fan-forced.
4 Spread pastry with pesto; top with tomatoes and olives. Sprinkle with cheese. Bake about 10 minutes. Drizzle with remaining oil before serving.

prep + cook time 30 minutes **serves** 4
nutritional count per serving 28.4g total fat (13.1g saturated fat); 1672kJ (400 cal); 22g carbohydrate; 13.5g protein; 2.9g fibre
tips Cherry tomatoes can be substituted for grape tomatoes, if you like. If you have some, scatter 2 teaspoons fresh thyme leaves over the tart just before serving.

spinach and beetroot tart

1 sheet puff pasty
250g frozen spinach, thawed, drained
1 cup (200g) fetta cheese, crumbled
½ x 850g can drained baby beetroot, sliced thinly

1 Preheat oven to 220°C/200°C fan-forced.
2 Place pastry on an oiled oven tray. Fold edges of pastry over to make a 5mm border all the way around pastry. Prick pastry base with fork. Place another oven tray on top of pastry; bake 10 minutes. Remove top tray from pastry. Reduce oven to 200°C/180°C fan-forced.
3 Meanwhile, combine spinach with half the cheese in medium bowl.
4 Top pastry with spinach mixture, beetroot and remaining cheese.
5 Bake tart about 10 minutes.

prep + cook time 40 minutes **serves** 4
nutritional count per serving 21.4g total fat (12.8g saturated fat); 1421kJ (340 cal); 22.1g carbohydrate; 13.4g protein; 4g fibre

spinach quiche

½ cup (80g) wholemeal self-raising flour
½ cup (80g) wholemeal plain flour
½ teaspoon salt
125g butter, chopped
2 teaspoons lemon juice
1 egg yolk
spinach filling
250g packet frozen chopped spinach
2 tablespoons olive oil
½ cup coarsely chopped green onions
¼ cup coarsely chopped fresh flat-leaf parsley
1 clove garlic, crushed
¼ teaspoon fresh dill
125g cottage cheese
125g fetta cheese
2 eggs, beaten lightly

1 Preheat oven to 200°C/180°C fan-forced.
2 Sift flours and salt into medium bowl, return husks from sifter to bowl; rub in butter. Add juice and egg yolk, combine until ingredients cling together. Knead gently on floured surface until smooth. Roll pastry between sheets of baking paper until large enough to line 23cm flan tin. Lift pastry into tin, gently press around base and side; trim edges. Bake about 15 minutes or until light golden brown; cool.
3 Reduce oven to 180°C/160°C fan-forced.
4 Meanwhile, make spinach filling.
5 Spread cold spinach filling into pastry case; bake about 30 minutes or until quiche is set.

spinach filling Put spinach in basin, allow to thaw; reserve liquid. Heat oil in frying pan; cook onion, parsley and garlic, stirring, until tender. Add spinach, reserved liquid and dill; cook, stirring constantly, over heat 2 minutes. Remove from heat; cool. When mixture is cold, stir in cheeses and eggs until well combined.

prep + cook time 45 minutes **serves** 6
nutritional count per serving 32.8g total fat (17g saturated fat); 1810kJ (433 cal); 17.9g carbohydrate; 14.9g protein; 5.3g fibre

fetta and prosciutto quiches

6 slices (150g) mountain bread
6 eggs
½ cup (125ml) milk
100g fetta cheese, crumbled
100g prosciutto, chopped coarsely
2 green onions, sliced thinly

1 Preheat oven to 170°C/150°C fan-forced. Oil six-hole (¾-cup/180ml)
texas muffin pan.
2 Cut a 17.5cm round from each slice of bread. Gently press rounds
into pan holes to make cups.
3 Whisk eggs and milk in large jug; stir in remaining ingredients. Pour
egg mixture into bread cups.
4 Bake quiches about 45 minutes or until set. Stand in pan 5 minutes.
Loosen quiches from edges of pan before lifting onto wire rack to cool.

prep + cook time 1 hour **makes** 6
nutritional count per quiche 11.9g total fat (5.3g saturated fat);
961kJ (230 cal); 13.6g carbohydrate; 17g protein; 1.2g fibre

shallot tartlets

1½ cups (225g) plain flour
125g butter
2 egg yolks
1 tablespoon water, approximately
1 egg white, beaten lightly
filling
60g butter
250g shallots, chopped finely
3 eggs, beaten lightly
300ml cream
30g blue cheese

1 Sift flour into bowl, rub in butter. Add egg yolks and enough water to make ingredients cling together. Press dough into a ball, cover; refrigerate 30 minutes.
2 Preheat oven to 200°C/180°C fan-forced.
3 Roll pastry until large enough to line six 11cm flan tins. Place tins on oven tray. Prick pastry all over with fork; bake about 15 minutes or until golden brown. Brush sides and bases with egg white; cool.
4 Reduce oven to 180°C/160°C fan-forced.
5 Meanwhile, make filling; pour into cases.
6 Bake tartlets about 15 minutes or until filling is set.
filling Heat butter in frying pan; cook shallots, stirring constantly, until soft; drain on absorbent paper. Cool. Combine egg, cream, crumbled cheese and shallot mixture in medium bowl.

prep + cook time 1 hour **makes** 6
nutritional count per tartlet 53.6g total fat (33.5g saturated fat); 2704kJ (647 cal); 30g carbohydrate; 12g protein; 1.8g fibre

lemon and mustard broccoli flan

1¼ cups (185g) plain flour
90g butter
1 egg yolk
1 tablespoon water, approximately
500g broccoli
6 green onions, sliced thinly
3 teaspoons finely grated lemon rind
1 tablespoon wholegrain mustard
300ml cream
3 eggs, beaten lightly
1 cup (120g) grated tasty cheese

1 Sift flour into bowl, rub in butter. Add egg yolk and enough water to make ingredients cling together. Knead gently on floured surface until smooth, cover; refrigerate 30 minutes.
2 Preheat oven to 200°C/180°C fan-forced.
3 Roll pastry until large enough to line deep 23cm flan tin. Ease pastry into flan tin, press into base and side; trim edges. Line pastry with baking paper, fill with dried beans or rice. Bake 7 minutes. Remove paper and beans; bake further 7 minutes or until golden brown. Cool.
4 Reduce oven to 180°C/160°C fan-forced.
5 Cut broccoli into small florets. Boil, steam or microwave until tender, drain; rinse under cold water, drain. Combine green onions, rind and mustard in small bowl. Heat cream in medium saucepan until nearly boiling, remove from heat, gradually whisk in egg.
6 Spread mustard mixture evenly over pastry, top with broccoli in single layer. Gradually pour egg mixture over broccoli, sprinkle with cheese. Bake about 40 minutes or until set and golden brown. Stand flan 5 minutes before serving.

prep + cook time 1 hour (+ refrigeration) **serves** 8
nutritional count per serving 45.1g total fat (27.9g saturated fat); 2391kJ (572 cal); 24.5g carbohydrate; 16.5g protein; 3.7g fibre

silver beet, cheese and fillo stacks

4 sheets fillo pastry
40g butter, melted
1 tablespoon olive oil
1 medium brown onion (150g), chopped finely
1 clove garlic, crushed
2 rindless bacon rashers (130g), chopped finely
1kg silver beet, trimmed, shredded finely
2 tablespoons lemon juice
200g ricotta cheese
100g fetta cheese, crumbled

1 Preheat oven to 200°C/180°C fan-forced. Grease oven trays.
2 Place one sheet of pastry on board; brush with butter, top with another pastry sheet. Repeat layering with pastry and butter. Cut pastry stack in half widthways; place on tray. Grease base of another similar-sized oven tray; place on top of pastry stack. Bake about 12 minutes or until browned. Cut each fillo stack into nine rectangles (you will have 18 in total).
3 Meanwhile, heat oil in large deep saucepan; cook onion, garlic and bacon, stirring, until onion softens and bacon is crisp. Add silver beet and juice; cook, covered, stirring occasionally, until silver beet is wilted and tender. Remove from heat; stir in cheeses.
4 Place one fillo rectangle on each serving plate; top equally with half the silver beet mixture then another fillo rectangle. Top with remaining silver beet mixture and remaining fillo rectangles.

prep + cook time 30 minutes **serves** 6
nutritional count per serving 19.6g total fat (10.1g saturated fat); 1162kJ (278 cal); 8.9g carbohydrate; 14.5g protein; 5.1g fibre

crab, fennel and herb quiches

3 sheets shortcrust pastry
1 tablespoon olive oil
1 medium fennel bulb (300g), sliced thinly
250g crab meat
2 tablespoons finely chopped fennel fronds
2 tablespoons finely chopped fresh flat-leaf parsley
½ cup (60g) coarsely grated cheddar cheese
quiche filling
300ml cream
¼ cup (60ml) milk
3 eggs

1 Preheat oven to 200°C/180°C fan-forced. Grease 12-hole (⅓-cup/80ml) muffin pan.
2 Cut twelve 9cm rounds from pastry; press into pan holes.
3 Heat oil in large frying pan; cook fennel, stirring, about 5 minutes or until fennel softens and browns slightly. Spoon fennel into pastry cases; top with combined crab, fronds, parsley and cheese.
4 Make quiche filling; pour into pastry cases.
5 Bake quiches about 25 minutes. Stand in pan 5 minutes before serving.
quiche filling Whisk ingredients in large jug.

prep + cook time 45 minutes **makes** 12
nutritional count per quiche 27.1g total fat (15g saturated fat); 1509kJ (361 cal); 20.3g carbohydrate; 9g protein; 1.3g fibre
tips We used lump crab meat from the fish market. Reserve fennel fronds when slicing the bulb.

caramelised leek and brie tartlets

1 tablespoon olive oil
25g butter
2 medium leeks (700g), sliced finely
1 clove garlic, crushed
1 tablespoon brown sugar
1 tablespoon white wine vinegar
3 sheets puff pastry
200g piece brie cheese
24 sprigs lemon thyme

1 Preheat oven to 200°C/180°C fan-forced. Grease two 12-hole
(2 tablespoons/40ml) deep flat-based patty pans.
2 Heat oil and butter in large frying pan; cook leek over medium heat,
stirring, about 5 minutes or until leek softens. Add garlic, sugar and
vinegar; cook, stirring, about 8 minutes or until leek caramelises.
3 Cut eight squares from each pastry sheet; press one pastry square
into each pan hole. Spoon leek mixture into pastry cases.
4 Cut cheese into 24 slices. Place a slice of cheese and thyme sprig
on top of each tartlet. Bake about 20 minutes.

prep + cook time 45 minutes **makes** 24
nutritional count per tartlet 8.8g total fat (4.8g saturated fat);
535kJ (128 cal); 8.7g carbohydrate; 3.1g protein; 0.8g fibre
tip We used an 8.5cm square cutter, measuring 8.5cm from corner to
corner, to make the pastry squares.

goats cheese and zucchini flower quiches

12 baby zucchini with flowers (240g)
3 sheets shortcrust pastry
100g firm goats cheese, chopped finely
⅓ cup (25g) finely grated parmesan cheese
2 tablespoons finely chopped garlic chives
quiche filling
300ml cream
¼ cup (60ml) milk
3 eggs

1 Preheat oven to 200°C/180°C fan-forced. Grease 12-hole (⅓-cup/80ml) muffin pan.
2 Remove flowers from zucchini; remove and discard stamens from flowers. Slice zucchini thinly.
3 Make quiche filling.
4 Cut twelve 9cm rounds from pastry; press into pan holes. Divide combined sliced zucchini, cheeses and chives into pastry cases; pour quiche filling into pastry cases. Top each quiche with a zucchini flower.
5 Bake quiches about 25 minutes. Stand in pan 5 minutes before serving.
quiche filling Whisk ingredients in large jug.

prep + cook time 1 hour **makes** 12
nutritional count per quiche 25.8g total fat (15g saturated fat); 1421kJ (340 cal); 19.9g carbohydrate; 7.1g protein; 1.1g fibre

prosciutto and roasted capsicum quiches

6 slices prosciutto (90g)
3 sheets shortcrust pastry
4 slices (170g) bottled roasted red capsicum, chopped coarsely
⅓ cup coarsely chopped fresh basil
¾ cup (75g) pizza cheese
quiche filling
300ml cream
¼ cup (60ml) milk
3 eggs

1 Preheat oven to 200°C/180°C fan-forced. Grease 12-hole (⅓-cup/80ml) muffin pan.
2 Cook prosciutto in heated oiled large frying pan until crisp. Cool; chop coarsely.
3 Make quiche filling.
4 Cut twelve 9cm rounds from pastry; press into pan holes. Divide combined prosciutto, capsicum, basil and cheese among pastry cases; pour quiche filling into pastry cases.
5 Bake quiches about 25 minutes. Stand in pan 5 minutes before serving.
quiche filling Whisk ingredients in large jug.

prep + cook time 45 minutes **makes** 12
nutritional count per quiche 26.5g total fat (14.8g saturated fat); 1462kJ (350 cal); 19.7g carbohydrate; 8.3g protein; 0.8g fibre

classic french onion tart

1½ cups (225g) plain flour
125g cold butter, chopped coarsely
1 egg yolk
2 tablespoons iced water, approximately
onion filling
60g butter
1 tablespoon olive oil
5 medium brown onions (750g), sliced thinly
pinch ground nutmeg
3 egg yolks
½ cup (125ml) pure cream

1 Process flour and butter until mixture is crumbly. Add egg yolk and enough of the water to process until ingredients just come together. Cover; refrigerate 30 minutes.
2 Preheat oven to 200°C/180°C fan-forced. Grease 22cm-round fluted loose-based flan tin.
3 Roll dough between sheets of baking paper until large enough to line tin. Lift pastry into tin, press into base and side, trim edge; prick base all over with fork. Place tin on oven tray; line pastry with baking paper, fill with dried beans or rice. Bake 10 minutes. Remove paper and beans; bake further 10 minutes. Cool.
4 Meanwhile, make onion filling.
5 Reduce oven temperature to 180°C/160°C fan-forced.
6 Spread onion mixture into tart shell. Bake about 25 minutes or until set.
onion filling Heat butter and oil in large frying pan; cook onion, covered, stirring occasionally, about 30 minutes or until onion is soft. Remove from heat. Add combined nutmeg, egg yolks and cream; mix well. Season with salt and cracked black pepper.

prep + cook time 1 hour 40 minutes (+ refrigeration & cooling)
serves 8
nutritional count per serving 31.4g total fat (18.2g saturated fat); 1726kJ (413 cal); 25.9g carbohydrate; 6.4g protein; 2.3g fibre

roast potato and bacon quiches

300g ruby lou potatoes, peeled, chopped coarsely
1 tablespoon olive oil
1 sheet puff pastry, thawed
2 teaspoons olive oil, extra
1 small brown onion (80g), sliced thinly
2 cloves garlic, crushed
3 rindless bacon rashers (195g), chopped coarsely
⅓ cup (80ml) milk
⅓ cup (80ml) cream
2 eggs
¼ cup (25g) coarsely grated mozzarella cheese

1 Preheat oven to 200°C/180°C fan-forced.
2 Place potato and oil in medium baking dish; stir to coat potato with oil. Roast about 30 minutes or until browned lightly and cooked through.
3 Meanwhile, cut pastry into four squares; gently press one square into each of four 1-cup (250ml) ovenproof dishes. Place dishes on oven tray; bake 10 minutes.
4 Heat extra oil in medium frying pan; cook onion, garlic and bacon, stirring, until onion softens and bacon is crisp. Drain on absorbent paper.
5 Divide potato among pastry shells; top with bacon mixture. Pour combined milk, cream, eggs and cheese into dishes.
6 Bake, uncovered, about 30 minutes or until filling sets. Stand quiches 5 minutes; carefully remove from dishes.

prep + cook time 1 hour 15 minutes **serves** 4
nutritional count per serving 36.7g total fat (12.2g saturated fat); 2161kJ (517 cal); 26.4g carbohydrate; 20.1g protein; 2.1g fibre
tip You can also use russet burbank or coliban potatoes for this recipe.

tomato, olive and ricotta tart

2 sheets puff pastry
¾ cup (110g) semi-dried tomatoes, chopped
¾ cup (90g) seeded black olives
½ cup (120g) ricotta cheese, crumbled
½ small red onion (50g), sliced
¼ cup fresh torn basil leaves
1 egg, beaten lightly

1 Preheat oven to 200°C/180°C fan-forced. Line oven tray with baking paper.
2 Cut a 16cm x 24cm rectangle from one pastry sheet; place on oven tray. Top with tomatoes, olives, cheese, onion and basil leaves.
3 Cut a 18cm x 24cm rectangle from remaining pastry sheet; score pastry in a diamond pattern then place on top of filling, press edges to seal. Brush with beaten egg.
4 Bake tart about 20 minutes.

prep + cook time 30 minutes **serves** 4
nutritional count per serving 25.1g total fat (12.5g saturated fat); 1965kJ (470 cal); 46.9g carbohydrate; 11.5g protein; 5.8g fibre

roasted capsicum and prosciutto tarts

6 slices prosciutto (90g)
3 sheets fillo pastry
cooking-oil spray
½ cup (120g) roasted red capsicum, chopped
¼ cup chopped fresh chives
5 eggs
⅓ cup (80ml) cream

1 Preheat oven to 200°C/180°C fan-forced. Grease six-hole (¾-cup/ 180ml) texas muffin pan.
2 Cook prosciutto in heated frying pan until crisp; chop coarsely.
3 Cut pastry sheets into six rectangles each (you will have 18 in total). Spray rectangles with oil; stack three rectangles on top of each other to make a star shape. Press pastry stars into pan holes. Divide capsicum, chives and prosciutto among pastry cases.
4 Whisk eggs and cream until combined; pour into pastry cases.
5 Bake tarts about 15 minutes.

prep + cook time 30 minutes **makes** 6
nutritional count per tart 13.9g total fat (5.9g saturated fat); 773kJ (185 cal); 4.7g carbohydrate; 10.5g protein; 0.2g fibre

goats cheese and asparagus tarts

3 sheets shortcrust pastry
20g butter
170g asparagus, trimmed, chopped finely
2 cloves garlic, crushed
1 tablespoon finely chopped fresh thyme leaves
150g goats cheese, crumbled
2 eggs, beaten lightly
⅔ cup (160ml) cream

1 Preheat oven to 200°C/180°C fan-forced. Oil two 12-hole
(2 tablespoons/40ml) patty pan trays.
2 Cut eight 7cm rounds from each pastry sheet; press rounds
firmly into pan holes.
3 Melt butter in small frying pan; cook asparagus, garlic and half
the thyme, stirring, about 5 minutes or until asparagus softens.
Divide asparagus mixture and cheese among pastry cases.
4 Combine egg and cream in small jug; pour over asparagus and
cheese mixture. Sprinkle remaining thyme over tarts.
5 Bake tarts 15 minutes.

prep + cook time 40 minutes **makes** 24
nutritional count per tart 10.7g total fat (6.2g saturated fat);
614kJ (147 cal); 9.6g carbohydrate; 3g protein; 0.5g fibre

213

smoked chicken and asparagus quiches

48 mini shortcrust pastry cases
5 medium asparagus spears (85g)
250g smoked chicken, chopped finely
2 tablespoons finely chopped fresh chives
4 eggs
⅔ cup (160ml) milk
½ cup (40g) finely grated parmesan cheese

1 Preheat oven to 200°C/180°C fan-forced. Return baked pastry cases to mini muffin pans.
2 Divide asparagus, chicken and chives into pastry cases.
3 Combine eggs and milk in large jug; pour into pastry cases, sprinkle with cheese.
4 Bake quiches about 10 minutes or until filling is set.

prep + cook time 30 minutes **makes** 48
nutritional count per quiche 3.6g total fat (1.8g saturated fat); 255kJ (61 cal); 4.1g carbohydrate; 2.9g protein; 0.2g fibre
tip These quiches are best served warm.

gluten-free egg and bacon pies

2 teaspoons vegetable oil
3 rindless bacon rashers (195g),
  chopped finely
1 small brown onion (80g),
  chopped finely
1 clove garlic, crushed
4 eggs
¼ cup (60ml) cream
¼ cup (20g) finely grated
  parmesan cheese
1 tablespoon finely chopped
  fresh chives

pastry
1 cup (180g) rice flour
¼ cup (35g) (corn) cornflour
¼ cup (30g) soya flour
¼ cup (20g) finely grated
  parmesan cheese
150g cold butter, chopped
2 tablespoons cold water,
  approximately

1 Make pastry.
2 Preheat oven to 220°C/200°C fan-forced. Oil six-hole (¾-cup/180ml)
texas muffin pan.
3 Roll pastry between sheets of baking paper until 5mm thick; cut six
11cm rounds from pastry. Ease pastry rounds into pan holes, press into
base and sides; prick bases with fork.
4 Bake pastry cases about 10 minutes or until browned lightly. Cool
cases in pan. Reduce oven to 200°C/180°C fan-forced.
5 Meanwhile, heat oil in small frying pan; cook bacon, onion and garlic,
stirring, until bacon is soft. Divide bacon mixture among pastry cases.
6 Whisk eggs and cream in medium jug; stir in cheese and chives. Fill
pastry cases with egg mixture. Bake about 25 minutes or until set.
pastry Process flours, cheese and butter until fine. Add enough of the
water to make ingredients come together. Cover; refrigerate 30 minutes.

prep + cook time 50 minutes (+ refrigeration and cooling) **makes** 6
nutritional count per pie 37.9g total fat (20.8g saturated fat);
2291kJ (548 cal); 54g carbohydrate; 17.6g protein; 1.5g fibre
tip This recipe is also wheat-free and yeast-free.

caramelised onion and goat cheese tartlets

1 cup (150g) plain flour
80g cold butter, chopped
1 egg yolk
2 tablespoons cold water
100g soft goat cheese
2 tablespoons coarsely
   chopped fresh chives

caramelised onion
2 tablespoons olive oil
4 large brown onions (800g),
   sliced thinly
⅓ cup (80ml) port
2 tablespoons red wine vinegar
2 tablespoons brown sugar

1 Blend or process flour and butter until mixture is crumbly. Add egg yolk and the water; process until ingredients come together. Enclose in plastic wrap; refrigerate 30 minutes.

2 Meanwhile, make caramelised onion.

3 Preheat oven to 200°C/180°C fan-forced. Grease four 10.5cm loose-based flan tins.

4 Divide pastry into four portions. Roll one portion of pastry between sheets of baking paper until large enough to line tin. Lift pastry into tin; press into side, trim edge, prick base all over with fork. Repeat with remaining pastry.

5 Place tins on oven tray; line pastry with baking paper, fill with dried beans or rice. Bake 10 minutes. Remove paper and beans; bake about 5 minutes or until tartlet shells brown lightly.

6 Divide onion mixture and cheese among tartlets. Bake about 5 minutes or until heated through. Sprinkle with chives.

caramelised onion Heat oil in large frying pan; cook onion, stirring, until onion softens. Add port, vinegar and sugar; cook, stirring occasionally, about 25 minutes or until onion caramelises.

prep + cook time 1 hour (+ refrigeration) **makes** 4
nutritional count per tartlet 31.5g total fat (15.2g saturated fat); 2165kJ (518 cal); 43.6g carbohydrate; 11g protein; 4g fibre

caramelised fennel tarts

50g butter
4 baby fennel bulbs (520g), trimmed, halved lengthways
1 teaspoon finely grated orange rind
½ cup (125ml) orange juice
1 sheet puff pastry
2 teaspoons finely chopped fresh thyme

1 Preheat oven to 220°C/200°C fan-forced. Grease two oven trays; line with baking paper.
2 Melt butter in large frying pan; cook fennel until browned lightly. Add rind and juice; bring to the boil. Reduce heat; simmer, uncovered, about 5 minutes or until fennel is caramelised and tender.
3 Cut pastry sheet into four squares; place on oven trays. Remove fennel from pan, leaving behind the pan juices; divide among pastry squares. Bake about 20 minutes or until pastry is browned.
4 Meanwhile, return pan juices to the boil. Reduce heat; simmer, uncovered, until sauce thickens slightly.
5 Serve tarts drizzled with sauce and sprinkled with thyme.

prep + cook time 45 minutes **makes** 4
nutritional count per tart 19.8g total fat (11.9g saturated fat); 1145kJ (274 cal); 19.9g carbohydrate; 3.3g protein; 2.7g fibre

creamy smoked salmon tartlets

3 sheets puff pastry
100g smoked salmon, chopped finely
2 gherkins, chopped finely
2 green onions, chopped finely
½ cup (120g) sour cream
1 tablespoon milk
2 eggs, beaten lightly
1 teaspoon finely chopped fresh dill
¼ teaspoon hot paprika

1 Preheat oven to 180°C/160°C fan-forced. Grease two 12-hole shallow patty pans.
2 Cut 24 x 6.5cm rounds from pastry; place into patty pan holes.
3 Sprinkle salmon, gherkin and onion into pastry cases; pour in combined sour cream, milk, egg, dill and paprika.
4 Bake tartlets about 30 minutes. Serve hot.

prep + cook time 45 minutes **makes** 24
nutritional count per tartlet 7.4g total fat (1.8g saturated fat); 464kJ (111 cal); 8.4g carbohydrate; 2.9g protein; 0.4g fibre

SWEET TARTS
& TARTLETS

banoffee pie

395g can sweetened condensed milk
75g butter, chopped
½ cup (110g) firmly packed brown sugar
2 tablespoons golden syrup
2 large bananas (460g), sliced thinly
300ml thickened cream, whipped
pastry
1½ cups (225g) plain flour
1 tablespoon icing sugar
140g cold butter, chopped
1 egg yolk
2 tablespoons cold water

1 Make pastry.
2 Grease 24cm-round loose-based fluted flan tin. Roll dough between sheets of baking paper until large enough to line tin. Ease dough into tin; press into base and side. Trim edge; prick base all over with fork. Cover; refrigerate 30 minutes.
3 Preheat oven to 200°C/180°C fan-forced.
4 Place tin on oven tray; line pastry with baking paper, fill with dried beans or rice. Bake 10 minutes; remove paper and beans. Bake 10 minutes; cool.
5 Meanwhile, cook condensed milk, butter, sugar and syrup in medium saucepan over medium heat, stirring, about 10 minutes or until mixture is caramel-coloured. Stand 5 minutes; pour into pie shell, cool.
6 Arrange banana slices on caramel; top with whipped cream.
pastry Process flour, sugar and butter until crumbly; add egg yolk and water, process until ingredients come together. Knead dough on floured surface until smooth. Enclose in plastic wrap; refrigerate 30 minutes.

prep + cook time 1 hour (+ refrigeration & standing) **serves** 8
nutritional count per serving 38.9g total fat (25.2g saturated fat); 2876kJ (688 cal); 77.5g carbohydrate; 9.7g protein; 1.9g fibre

lemon chiffon pie

1¾ cups (180g) plain sweet biscuit crumbs
125g butter, melted
filling
4 eggs, separated
⅓ cup (75g) caster sugar
3 teaspoons gelatine
2 teaspoons grated lemon rind
⅓ cup (80ml) lemon juice
⅓ cup (80ml) water
⅓ cup (75g) caster sugar, extra

1 Combine biscuit crumbs and butter in medium bowl. Press mixture firmly over base and side of 23cm pie plate; refrigerate 30 minutes or until firm.
2 Meanwhile, make filling.
3 Spread filling into crumb crust; refrigerate several hours or until set.
filling Stir egg yolks, caster sugar, gelatine, rind, juice and the water in medium heatproof bowl over medium saucepan of simmering water until mixture has thickened slightly. Remove from heat; pour into large bowl. Cover; cool to room temperature. Mixture should be set to about the consistency of unbeaten egg white before remaining ingredients are added. Beat egg whites in small bowl with electric mixer until soft peaks form; add extra sugar gradually, beating until dissolved after additions. Fold egg white mixture through lemon mixture in two batches.

prep + cook time 40 minutes (+ refrigeration & standing) **serves** 8
nutritional count per serving 19.4g total fat (11.1g saturated fat); 1409kJ (337 cal); 35.1g carbohydrate; 6.4g protein; 0.5g fibre

key lime pie

150g granita biscuits
80g butter, melted
4 egg yolks
400g can sweetened condensed milk
1 tablespoon finely grated lime rind
½ cup (125ml) lime juice
300ml thickened cream, whipped

1 Preheat oven to 180°C/160°C fan-forced.
2 Process or blend biscuits until fine, transfer to small bowl; stir in butter. Press mixture over base and side of 23cm pie plate. Place plate on oven tray; bake 10 minutes. Cool.
3 Beat egg yolks in small bowl with electric mixer until light and fluffy. Beat in condensed milk, rind and juice on low speed. Pour mixture into crumb crust.
4 Bake pie about 12 minutes or until barely set. Refrigerate 3 hours before serving. Serve pie with cream or ice cream.

prep + cook time 45 minutes (+ refrigeration) **serves** 8
nutritional count per serving 30.1g total fat (18.2 g saturated fat); 1998 kJ (478 cal); 42.9g carbohydrate; 8.7g protein; 1.1g fibre
tip If you like, use green food colouring to tint the pie filling.

treacle tart

1¼ cups (185g) plain flour
⅓ cup (40g) custard powder
2 tablespoons icing sugar
125g butter, chopped
2 tablespoons milk, approximately
filling
1½ cups (100g) stale breadcrumbs
1 cup (360g) treacle
2 teaspoons grated lemon rind

1 Sift flour, custard powder and icing sugar into medium bowl, rub in butter. Add enough milk to make ingredients cling together. Press dough into a ball; knead gently on floured surface until smooth. Cover; refrigerate 30 minutes.
2 Preheat oven to 200°C/180°C fan-forced.
3 Roll two-thirds of the dough between sheets of baking paper until large enough to line 22cm flan tin. Lift pastry into tin, ease into base and side; trim edge. Place tin on oven tray, line pastry with paper, fill with dried beans or rice. Bake 10 minutes. Remove paper and beans; bake further 10 minutes or until lightly browned. Cool.
4 Reduce oven to 180°C/160°C fan-forced.
5 Make filling; spread into pastry case.
6 Roll remaining pastry into a rectangle on floured surface; cut into 1cm strips. Brush edge of pastry case with a little extra milk. Place pastry strips over filling in lattice pattern; brush pastry with a little more milk.
7 Bake tart 25 minutes or until pastry is lightly browned. Cool tart in tin. Just before serving, dust with icing sugar, if you like. Serve with whipped cream or ice-cream.
filling Combine all ingredients in medium bowl.

prep + cook time 1 hour (+ refrigeration & standing) **serves** 8
nutritional count per serving 13.8g total fat (8.7g saturated fat); 1618kJ (387 cal); 61.6g carbohydrate; 4.9g protein; 1.8g fibre

chocolate-brownie caramel tart

1 cup (150g) plain flour
100g cold unsalted butter,
    chopped
¼ cup (55g) caster sugar
½ cup (75g) finely chopped
    macadamias
1 egg yolk
1 tablespoon icing sugar

caramel filling
60g unsalted butter
400g can sweetened
    condensed milk
1 tablespoon golden syrup
2 tablespoons cream
chocolate-brownie topping
80g unsalted butter
½ cup (110g) caster sugar
70g dark chocolate, chopped
1 egg, beaten lightly
¼ cup (35g) plain flour
1 tablespoon cocoa powder

1 Grease 24cm round loose-based flan tin. Process flour and butter until crumbly, add sugar, nuts and egg yolk, process until ingredients just cling together. Knead dough on floured surface until smooth. Press dough over base and side of tin; prick base with fork. Cover; refrigerate 30 minutes.
2 Preheat oven to 200°C/180°C fan-forced.
3 Line pastry with baking paper large enough to extend 10cm over edge, tuck paper under tin to completely cover pastry; fill with dried beans or rice. Place tin on oven tray, bake 15 minutes. Remove beans and paper, loosely cover top edge of pastry with greased foil; bake further 8 minutes or until pastry is lightly browned. Cool.
4 Meanwhile, make caramel filling. Spread warm filling into cool pastry case; stand 30 minutes or until cold and firm.
5 Reduce oven to 180°C/160°C fan-forced.
6 Make chocolate-brownie topping. Pour topping over caramel; bake about 1 hour. Cool tart in tin. Cover; refrigerate 4 hours. Serve with cream.
caramel filling Stir ingredients in small saucepan over medium heat about 10 minutes, until caramel becomes golden brown. Cool slightly.
chocolate-brownie topping Melt butter in small saucepan, add sugar; stir over heat, without boiling, until sugar dissolves. Remove from heat; stir in chocolate until melted, then stir in egg, sifted flour and cocoa. Cool.

prep + cook time 1 hour 40 minutes (+ refrigeration) **serves** 10
nutritional count per serving 34.5g total fat (19.1g saturated fat); 2387kJ (571 cal); 60.2g carbohydrate; 7.6g protein; 1.3g fibre

baked passionfruit tart

1½ cups (225g) plain flour
⅓ cup (55g) icing sugar
150g cold unsalted butter, chopped
2 egg yolks
filling
7 egg yolks
1 cup (220g) caster sugar
1 teaspoon finely grated lemon rind
⅓ cup (80ml) passionfruit pulp
1 cup (250ml) thickened cream

1 Process flour, sugar and butter until crumbly. Add egg yolks, process until ingredients just come together. Knead dough on floured surface until smooth. Wrap in plastic; refrigerate 30 minutes.
2 Roll pastry between sheets of baking paper until large enough to line 24cm round loose-based flan tin. Ease pastry into base and side of tin; trim edge. Cover; refrigerate 1 hour.
3 Preheat oven to 200°C/180°C fan-forced.
4 Line pastry with baking paper, fill with dried beans or rice. Place tin on oven tray; bake 10 minutes. Remove paper and beans; bake further 10 minutes or until pastry is lightly browned. Cool.
5 Reduce oven to 150°C/130°C fan-forced.
6 Make filling; pour into pastry case. Bake tart about 1 hour or until just set; cool. Serve at room temperature, dusted with a little sifted icing sugar, if you like.
filling Combine all ingredients in medium bowl.

prep + cook time 1 hour 30 minutes (+ refrigeration & standing)
serves 8
nutritional count per serving 33g total fat (19.6g saturated fat); 2282kJ (546 cal); 56.3g carbohydrate; 7.1g protein; 2.5g fibre
tip You need about 4 passionfruit for this recipe.

237

crème brûlée tart

1½ cups (225g) plain flour
2 tablespoons custard powder
125g cold butter, chopped
1 egg yolk
1 tablespoon cold water,
  approximately

filling
5 egg yolks
⅓ cup (75g) caster sugar
1 vanilla bean
1½ cups (375ml) thickened cream
⅓ cup (80ml) milk
topping
1½ tablespoons brown sugar
1 tablespoon pure icing sugar

1 Grease 24cm round loose-based flan tin. Process flour, custard powder and butter until just crumbly. Add egg yolk and enough water to make ingredients just cling together. Press dough into a ball, knead on floured surface until smooth. Wrap in plastic wrap; refrigerate 30 minutes.
2 Roll pastry between sheets of baking paper until large enough to line tin. Lift pastry into tin, ease into base and side; trim edge. Refrigerate 30 minutes.
3 Preheat oven to 200°C/180°C fan-forced.
4 Line pastry with baking paper, fill with dried beans or rice; place on oven tray. Bake 10 minutes. Remove paper and beans; bake further 10 minutes or until pastry is lightly browned. Cool.
5 Reduce oven to 150°C/130°C fan-forced.
6 Meanwhile, make filling. Pour filling into pastry case. Bake tart about 1 hour or until custard is set; cool.
7 Make topping. Sift topping evenly over filling; refrigerate 1 hour.
8 Preheat grill. Cover pastry edge of tart with foil; place under hot grill 2 minutes or until sugar is melted and golden brown. (If sugar does not melt in 2 minutes, lightly brush topping with water and grill again.)
filling Whisk egg yolks and sugar in medium bowl until thick and creamy. Split vanilla bean lengthways, scrape seeds into medium saucepan. Bring cream and milk to the boil in small saucepan; remove from heat. Whisk hot milk mixture into egg yolk mixture; strain. Cool.
topping Sift sugars together twice through a fine sieve.

prep + cook time 1 hour 40 minutes (+ refrigeration & standing) **serves** 8
nutritional count per serving 34.6g total fat (21.3g saturated fat); 2023kJ (484 cal); 37.8g carbohydrate; 6.5g protein; 1.1g fibre

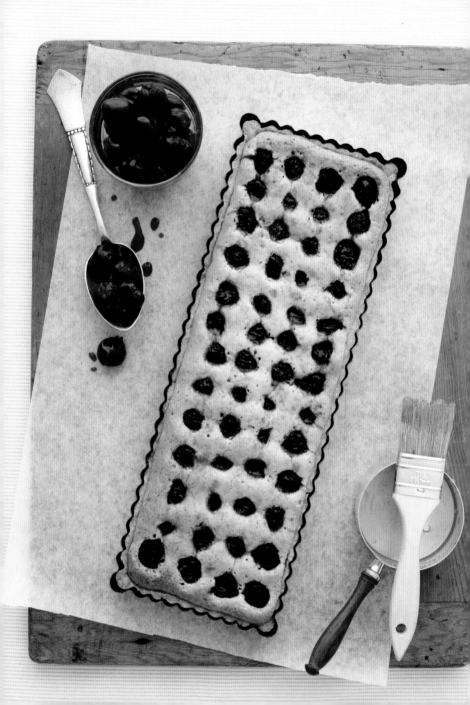

cherry almond tart

1 cup (150g) plain flour
½ cup (35g) rice flour
2 tablespoons caster sugar
90g cold butter, chopped
1 egg, beaten lightly
2 teaspoons cold water,
    approximately

filling
70g butter
½ cup (75g) caster sugar
1 egg
⅔ cup (80g) ground almonds
1 tablespoon plain flour
500g fresh cherries, seeded
glaze
2 tablespoons apricot jam
1 tablespoon water

1 Grease 11cm x 35cm rectangular or 20cm round loose-based flan tin.
Sift flours and sugar into medium bowl; rub in butter. Add egg and enough
water to make ingredients cling together. Knead dough on floured
surface until smooth. Cover with plastic wrap; refrigerate 30 minutes.
2 Roll pastry between sheets of baking paper until large enough to line
tin. Lift pastry into tin, ease into base and sides; trim edges. Lightly prick
base with fork; refrigerate 30 minutes.
3 Preheat oven to 200°C/180°C fan-forced.
4 Line pastry with baking paper; fill with dried beans or rice. Place tin
on oven tray; bake10 minutes. Remove paper and beans; bake another
10 minutes or until pastry is lightly browned. Cool.
5 Reduce oven to 180°C/160°C fan-forced.
6 Meanwhile, make filling. Spread filling into pastry case; top with cherries,
pressing gently into almond mixture. Bake about 40 minutes; cool.
7 Make glaze; brush tart evenly with hot glaze.
filling Beat butter, sugar and egg in small bowl with electric mixer until
light and fluffy. Add almonds, beat until thick; stir in flour.
glaze Stir ingredients in small saucepan over heat until mixture comes
to the boil; strain.

prep + cook time 1 hour 30 minutes (+ refrigeration & standing)
serves 6
nutritional count per serving 31.7g total fat (15.6g saturated fat);
2278kJ (545 cal); 55.9g carbohydrate; 9.2g protein; 3.4g fibre
tip You can use canned cherries if fresh are not in season.

linzer torte

1 cup (150g) plain flour
½ cup (75g) self-raising flour
½ teaspoon ground cinnamon
¼ teaspoon ground nutmeg
60g ground almonds
2 tablespoons sugar
125g butter, chopped
1 egg yolk
2 tablespoons water, approximately
1 cup (320g) raspberry jam

1 Preheat oven to 180°C/160°C fan-forced.
2 Sift flours and spices into medium bowl, add almonds and sugar; rub in butter until mixture resembles fine breadcrumbs. Add egg yolk and enough of the water to mix to a firm dough. Knead dough on floured surface until smooth.
3 Roll two-thirds of the pastry thinly between sheets of baking paper, large enough to fit 23cm flan tin. Lift pastry into tin, ease into base and side; trim edge. Spread base with jam.
4 Roll remaining pastry between sheets of baking paper, cut into 1cm strips. Arrange pastry strips in a lattice pattern over jam.
5 Bake torte about 45 minutes or until pastry is lightly browned. Serve torte warm or cold.

prep + cook time 1 hour 15 minutes **serves** 8
nutritional count per serving 17.9g total fat (8.9g saturated fat); 1605kJ (384 cal); 51.1g carbohydrate; 5g protein; 2.2g fibre

italian ricotta cheesecake

90g butter, softened
¼ cup (55g) caster sugar
1 egg
1¼ cups (185g) plain flour
¼ cup (35g) self-raising flour
filling
1kg ricotta cheese
1 tablespoon finely grated lemon rind
¼ cup (60ml) lemon juice
1 cup (220g) caster sugar
5 eggs
¼ cup (40g) sultanas
¼ cup (80g) finely chopped glacé fruit salad

1 Beat butter, sugar and egg in small bowl with electric mixer until
combined. Stir in half the sifted flours; then work in remaining flour with
hand. Knead pastry on floured surface until smooth. Wrap in plastic;
refrigerate 30 minutes.
2 Grease 28cm springform tin. Press pastry over base of tin; prick
with fork. Place on oven tray; refrigerate 30 minutes.
3 Preheat oven to 200°C/180°C fan-forced.
4 Line pastry with baking paper, fill with dried beans or rice; bake
10 minutes. Remove paper and beans; bake further 15 minutes or
until browned lightly. Cool.
5 Reduce oven to 160°C/140°C fan-forced.
6 Make filling; pour into tin.
7 Bake cheesecake about 50 minutes; cool in oven with door ajar.
Refrigerate 3 hours or overnight. Serve dusted with icing sugar, if you like.
filling Process cheese, rind, juice, sugar and eggs until smooth; transfer
to large bowl. Stir in fruit.

prep + cook time 1 hour 30 minutes (+ refrigeration & standing)
serves 16
nutritional count per serving 13.8g total fat (8.2g saturated fat);
1262kJ (302 cal); 33.2g carbohydrate; 10.7g protein; 0.7g fibre

chocolate almond tart

50g dark eating chocolate, chopped coarsely
¼ cup (55g) caster sugar
1 tablespoon cocoa powder
½ cup (60g) ground almonds
20g cold unsalted butter, chopped finely
2 teaspoons brandy
2 eggs
2 sheets puff pastry

1 Process chocolate, sugar, cocoa and ground nuts until chocolate is chopped finely. Add butter and process until mixture begins to come together. Add brandy and 1 egg; process to combine.
2 Cut one pastry sheet into 12cm x 24cm rectangle; cut the other into 14cm x 24cm rectangle. Leaving a 2cm border along all sides, cut even slits in centre of larger pastry sheet at 1.5cm intervals. Place smaller sheet on greased oven tray; spread centre with chocolate mixture, leaving a 2cm border. Brush edges with a little of the remaining beaten egg.
3 Top with other pastry sheet, press edges together. Freeze 10 minutes.
4 Preheat oven to 200°C/180°C fan-forced.
5 Brush pastry lightly with remaining beaten egg; bake about 35 minutes or until golden.

prep + cook time 1 hour (+ freezing) **serves** 4
nutritional count per serving 38.2g total fat (7.8g saturated fat); 2541kJ (608 cal); 52.7g carbohydrate; 12.5g protein; 2.7g fibre

mango galettes with coconut cream

1 sheet puff pastry, quartered
20g butter, melted
2 firm medium mangoes (860g), halved, sliced thinly
1 tablespoon brown sugar
⅔ cup (160ml) thickened cream, whipped
2 teaspoons coconut-flavoured liqueur
⅓ cup (15g) flaked coconut, toasted

1 Preheat oven to 200°C/180°C fan-forced. Grease oven tray; line with baking paper.
2 Place pastry squares on oven tray, prick with fork; brush with half the melted butter. Divide mango among pastry squares, leaving 2cm border. Sprinkle sugar over galettes; drizzle with remaining butter.
3 Bake galettes about 15 minutes.
4 Meanwhile, combine remaining ingredients in small bowl.
5 Serve galettes with coconut cream.

prep + cook time 30 minutes **serves** 4
nutritional count per serving 31.2g total fat (19.7g saturated fat); 1969kJ (471 cal); 40.1g carbohydrate; 5g protein; 3.4g fibre

french apple flan

90g butter, softened
¼ cup (55g) caster sugar
1 egg
1¼ cups (185g) plain flour
¼ cup (35g) self-raising flour
375ml jar apple sauce
2 large apples (400g)
1 teaspoon grated lemon rind
2 tablespoons lemon juice
2 tablespoons apricot jam
1 tablespoon brandy

1 Beat butter in small bowl with electric mixture until smooth; beat in sugar and egg until just combined. Stir in sifted flours, in two batches, until ingredients just cling together. Knead gently on floured surface until smooth (over-handling of this pastry will cause it to toughen and crack when rolled out). Wrap pastry in plastic wrap; refrigerate 30 minutes.
2 Roll pastry between baking paper until large enough to line 23cm flan tin. Ease pastry into tin, press into base and side; trim edge with rolling pin. Refrigerate 30 minutes.
3 Preheat oven to 200°C/180°C fan-forced.
4 Line pastry with baking paper; fill with dried beans or rice. Bake 7 minutes. Remove paper and beans; bake further 10 minutes or until lightly browned. Cool.
5 Reduce oven to 200°C/180°C fan-forced.
6 Spread apple sauce into pastry case. Peel and core apples, cut into wedges. Slice wedges thinly, toss apple slices in combined rind and juice. Overlap apple slices evenly over apple sauce.
7 Bake flan about 30 minutes or until apples are tender. Combine jam and brandy in small saucepan, stir over low heat until warm; strain. Brush over apples; serve warm or cold.

prep + cook time 1 hour (+ refrigeration) **serves** 6
nutritional count per serving 13.9g total fat (8.5g saturated fat); 1676kJ (401 cal); 61.5g carbohydrate; 5.6g protein; 3.3g fibre
tips Flan can be made the day before; keep covered in refrigerator. We used granny smith apples in this recipe.

apple cinnamon tarts

1 large golden delicious apple (200g)
1 sheet sweet puff pastry
20g butter, melted
1 teaspoon cinnamon sugar
¼ cup (80g) apricot jam, warmed

1 Preheat oven to 220°C/200°C fan-forced. Grease oven tray.
2 Peel, core and halve apple; slice thinly.
3 Cut pastry sheet in half to form two rectangles; place on tray.
Overlap apple slices down centre of pastry halves. Brush apple
with butter; sprinkle with cinnamon sugar.
4 Bake tarts about 15 minutes or until pastry is browned.
Brush tarts with jam.

prep + cook time 30 minutes **serves** 4
nutritional count per serving 13.6g total fat (3.4g saturated fat);
1120kJ (268 cal); 34g carbohydrate; 2.5g protein; 1.5g fibre

gluten-free chocolate tart

⅓ cup (110g) strawberry jam
⅔ cup (160ml) cream
25g unsalted butter
200g dark eating chocolate, chopped finely
6 strawberries, halved
hazelnut crust
1½ cups (150g) ground hazelnuts
⅓ cup (75g) caster sugar
¼ cup (35g) (corn) cornflour
125g cold unsalted butter, chopped
1 egg yolk

1 Make hazelnut crust.
2 Grease 22cm-round loose-based flan tin. Roll hazelnut dough between sheets of baking paper until large enough to line tin. Ease dough into tin, press into base and side; trim edge. Cover; refrigerate 30 minutes.
3 Preheat oven to 200°C/180°C fan-forced.
4 Place tin on oven tray. Bake hazelnut crust about 25 minutes. Spread jam over crust; return to oven 2 minutes. Cool.
5 Heat cream in medium saucepan; remove from heat, stir in butter and chocolate, then whisk until smooth. Pour chocolate mixture into crust; refrigerate 2 hours. Top tart with strawberries.
hazelnut crust Process ground hazelnuts, sugar, cornflour and butter until crumbly; add egg yolk, pulse until mixture comes together. Knead dough gently on floured surface until smooth. Wrap in plastic; refrigerate 1 hour.

prep + cook time 50 minutes (+ refrigeration) **serves** 12
nutritional count per serving 29.1g total fat (14g saturated fat); 1597kJ (382 cal); 26.6g carbohydrate; 3.4g protein; 1.8g fibre
tip This recipe is also wheat-free and yeast-free.

macadamia golden syrup tart

1¼ cups (185g) plain flour
½ cup (80g) icing sugar
90g butter, chopped
1 egg yolk
2 teaspoons water, approximately
2 eggs, beaten lightly, extra
⅓ cup (80ml) golden syrup
60g butter, melted
⅓ cup (75g) firmly packed brown sugar
1½ cups (200g) roasted macadamias, chopped coarsely
1 tablespoon golden syrup, extra

1 Sift flour and icing sugar into medium bowl; rub in butter (Or, process flour, icing sugar and butter until crumbly.) Add egg yolk and enough water to form a soft dough. Knead pastry gently until smooth. Cover; refrigerate 1 hour.
2 Roll pastry on floured surface until large enough to line 13cm x 36cm loose-based rectangular flan tin. Ease pastry into tin, press into sides; trim edges. Cover; refrigerate 30 minutes.
3 Preheat oven to 180°C/160°C fan-forced. Place tin on oven tray.
4 Line pastry case with baking paper, fill with dried beans or rice. Bake 15 minutes. Remove paper and beans; bake about 5 minutes or until browned lightly.
5 Whisk eggs, syrup, butter and brown sugar in small bowl until smooth; stir in nuts. Pour mixture into pastry case.
6 Bake tart about 25 minutes or until set. Cool. Brush with extra syrup.

prep + cook time 1 hour (+ refrigeration) **serves** 8
nutritional count per serving 36.8g total fat (13.4g saturated fat); 2299kJ (550 cal); 49.5g carbohydrate; 6.8g protein; 2.4g fibre
tip Use regular golden syrup for this recipe, not the squeezable bottles, as this has a lighter texture.

almond, date and pistachio tart

1 cup (150g) plain flour
⅓ cup (55g) icing sugar
90g cold butter, chopped
1 egg yolk
1 tablespoon cold water,
  approximately
300g fresh dates
¼ cup (80g) fig jam, warmed
⅓ cup (70g) roasted pistachios

frangipane
100g butter, softened
1 teaspoon finely grated lemon rind
½ cup (110g) caster sugar
1 egg
2 tablespoons plain flour
¾ cup (90g) ground almonds

1 Blend or process flour, sugar and butter until combined. Add egg yolk and enough water to make ingredients just come together. Knead dough on floured surface until smooth. Cover; refrigerate 30 minutes.
2 Preheat oven to 180°C/160°C fan-forced. Grease 23cm loose-based flan tin.
3 Roll pastry between sheets of baking paper until large enough to line tin. Ease pastry into tin, press into sides; trim edge. Line pastry case with baking paper, fill with dried beans or rice; place on oven tray. Bake 15 minutes. Remove paper and beans; wrap strip of foil around edges of tin to protect sides from over-browning. Bake 15 minutes or until pastry base is browned.
4 Meanwhile, make frangipane.
5 Split dates in half; remove seeds. Place dates, cut-side down, on base of pastry case. Spread frangipane mixture over dates.
6 Bake tart about 30 minutes or until browned and set. Cool. Brush tart with warmed jam and sprinkle with pistachios just before serving.
frangipane Beat butter, rind and sugar in small bowl with electric mixer until creamy. Beat in egg, flour and ground nuts until combined.

prep + cook time 1 hour (+ refrigeration) **serves** 8
nutritional count per serving 31.5g total fat (14.2g saturated fat); 2199kJ (526 cal); 53g carbohydrate; 8.1g protein; 4g fibre

chocolate pistachio tart

½ cup (70g) roasted, unsalted
   pistachios
100g unsalted butter, softened
½ cup (110g) caster sugar
2 eggs
⅔ cup (100g) self-raising flour
⅓ cup (35g) cocoa powder
½ cup (160g) raspberry jam
12 roasted, unsalted pistachios,
   extra
40g dark chocolate Melts, melted

pastry
1¼ cups (185g) plain flour
½ cup (80g) icing sugar
125g cold unsalted butter,
   chopped coarsely
2 tablespoons iced water,
   approximately

1 Make pastry; cover, refrigerate 30 minutes.
2 Grease 12.5cm x 35cm (or 22cm round) loose-based fluted flan tin.
Reserve one-quarter of the dough for decoration. Roll remaining dough
between sheets of baking paper until large enough to line tin. Ease
dough into tin; press into base and sides. Trim edges; prick base all over
with a fork. Refrigerate 30 minutes.
3 Roll out reserved dough on a floured surface, cut out 12 x 2cm rounds;
place on a tray lined with baking paper. Refrigerate 30 minutes.
4 Preheat oven to 200°C/180°C fan-forced.
5 Blend or process nuts finely.
6 Beat butter and sugar in small bowl with electric mixer until light and
fluffy. Beat in eggs, one at a time. Transfer mixture to medium bowl; stir
in sifted flour and cocoa, and nuts. Spread jam over base of pastry case;
top with pistachio filling. Place pastry rounds on filling. Bake 15 minutes.
7 Reduce oven to 180°C/160°C fan-forced; bake further 25 minutes.
Cool in pan.
8 Dip extra nuts in chocolate; place on pastry rounds. Cool before slicing.
pastry Process sifted flour and sugar with butter until crumbly. Add
enough of the water until ingredients just come together when processed.
Knead dough on floured surface until smooth.

prep + cook time 1 hour 15 minutes (+ refrigeration) **serves** 12
nutritional count per serving 21.4g total fat (11.8g saturated fat);
1655kJ (396 cal); 45.6g carbohydrate; 6g protein; 1.9g fibre

tarte tatin

6 large apples (1.2kg)
100g unsalted butter, chopped
1 cup (220g) firmly packed brown sugar
2 tablespoons lemon juice
pastry
1 cup (150g) plain flour
2 tablespoons caster sugar
80g cold unsalted butter, chopped
2 tablespoons sour cream

1 Peel, core and quarter apples. Melt butter in large heavy-based frying pan; add apple, sprinkle evenly with sugar and juice. Cook, uncovered, over low heat, 1 hour, turning apple as it caramelises.

2 Place apple, rounded-sides down, in 23cm pie dish; drizzle with 1 tablespoon of the caramel. Reserve remaining caramel in pan. Pack apples into dish tightly to avoid any gaps. Cover; refrigerate until required.

3 Make pastry; cover, refrigerate 30 minutes.

4 Preheat oven to 200°C/180°C fan-forced.

5 Roll dough between sheets of baking paper until large enough to cover apple. Peel away one sheet of baking paper; invert pastry over apple. Remove remaining paper; tuck pastry around apple.

6 Bake tart about 30 minutes or until browned. Carefully turn onto serving plate. Reheat reserved caramel over low heat; drizzle over apple. Serve with cream or ice-cream, if you like.

pastry Process flour, sugar, butter and sour cream until ingredients just come together. Knead dough on floured surface until smooth.

prep + cook time 2 hours (+ refrigeration) **serves** 8
nutritional count per serving 21.1g total fat (13.7g saturated fat); 1781kJ (426 cal); 57.5g carbohydrate; 2.7g protein; 2.8g fibre

lime meringue pie

250g plain sweet biscuits
100g unsalted butter, melted
½ cup (75g) wheaten cornflour
1½ cups (330g) caster sugar
½ cup (125ml) lime juice
1¼ cups (310ml) water
60g unsalted butter, extra
4 eggs, separated
2 teaspoons finely grated lime rind

1 Grease 24cm-round loose-based flan tin.
2 Blend or process biscuits until mixture resembles fine breadcrumbs. Add butter; process until combined. Press biscuit mixture evenly over base and 2cm up the side of tin; place on oven tray. Refrigerate until required.
3 Combine cornflour and ½ cup of the sugar in medium saucepan; gradually stir in juice and the water until smooth. Cook, stirring, over high heat until mixture boils and thickens. Reduce heat; simmer, stirring, 1 minute. Remove from heat; stir in extra butter, then yolks and rind. Continue stirring until butter melts. Cool 10 minutes.
4 Spread filling over biscuit base. Cover; refrigerate 2 hours.
5 Preheat oven to 200°C/180°C fan-forced.
6 Beat egg whites in small bowl with electric mixer until soft peaks form; gradually add remaining sugar, 1 tablespoon at a time, beating until sugar dissolves between additions.
7 Roughen surface of filling with a fork before spreading with meringue mixture. Bake about 5 minutes or until meringue is browned lightly.

prep + cook time 30 minutes (+ refrigeration) **serves** 10
nutritional count per serving 19.8g total fat (11.5g saturated fat); 1756kJ (420 cal); 57.3g carbohydrate; 4.8g protein; 0.6g fibre

chocolate tart

1½ cups (225g) plain flour
½ cup (110g) caster sugar
140g cold butter, chopped coarsely
1 egg, beaten lightly
1 teaspoon cocoa powder
chocolate filling
2 eggs
2 egg yolks
¼ cup (55g) caster sugar
250g dark eating chocolate, melted
200g butter, melted

1 Process flour, sugar and butter until crumbly; add egg, process until ingredients come together. Knead dough on floured surface until smooth. Enclose in plastic wrap; refrigerate 30 minutes.
2 Roll pastry between sheets of baking paper until large enough to line greased 24cm-round loose-based flan tin. Lift pastry into tin; press into base and side, trim edge, prick base all over with fork. Cover; refrigerate 30 minutes.
3 Meanwhile, preheat oven to 200°C/180°C fan-forced.
4 Make chocolate filling.
5 Place flan tin on oven tray; cover pastry with baking paper, fill with dried beans or rice. Bake 10 minutes. Remove paper and beans carefully from tin; bake about 5 minutes or until pastry has browned lightly. Cool.
6 Reduce oven to 180°C/160°C fan-forced.
7 Pour chocolate filling into pastry case. Bake about 10 minutes or until filling has set; cool 10 minutes. Refrigerate 1 hour. Serve dusted with sifted cocoa powder. Serve tart topped with strawberries, if you like..
chocolate filling Whisk eggs, egg yolks and sugar in medium heatproof bowl over medium saucepan of simmering water (don't let water touch base of bowl) about 15 minutes or until light and fluffy. Gently whisk chocolate and butter into egg mixture.

prep + cook time 1 hour 30 minutes (+ refrigeration) **serves** 8
nutritional count per serving 48.1g total fat (32.7g saturated fat); 2934kJ (702 cal); 59.1g carbohydrate; 7.9g protein; 2.5g fibre

vanilla cheesecake with poached quinces

125g granita biscuits
80g butter, melted
1 vanilla bean
2 x 250g packets cream cheese,
   softened
2 eggs
½ cup (120g) sour cream

¼ cup (60ml) lemon juice
2⅔ cups (590g) caster sugar
2 cups (500ml) water
2 medium quinces (660g),
   peeled, cored, quartered
2 strips lemon rind

1 Preheat oven to 160°C/140°C fan-forced. Insert base of 23cm springform tin upside down in tin to give a flat base; grease tin.
2 Blend or process biscuits until mixture resembles fine breadcrumbs. Add butter; process until combined. Press biscuit mixture evenly over base of tin. Cover; refrigerate about 30 minutes or until firm.
3 Meanwhile, split vanilla bean in half lengthways, scrape seeds into medium bowl; reserve pod for poached quinces. Add cheese, eggs, sour cream, juice and ⅔ cup of the sugar to seeds; beat with electric mixer until smooth.
4 Place tin on oven tray; pour in cheesecake mixture. Bake about 35 minutes or until set. Turn oven off; cool cheesecake in oven with door ajar. Cover; refrigerate overnight.
5 Meanwhile, stir the water and remaining sugar in medium saucepan over low heat until sugar dissolves. Add quince, rind and reserved vanilla pod; bring to the boil. Reduce heat; simmer, covered, about 2 hours or until quince is tender and rosy in colour. Cool quince in syrup; slice thinly.
6 Return quince syrup to the boil. Reduce heat; simmer, uncovered, until syrup reduces by half; cool. Top cheesecake with quince slices; brush with syrup.

prep + cook time 2 hours (+ refrigeration) **serves** 12
nutritional count per serving 26.1g total fat (16.2g saturated fat); 2094kJ (501 cal); 61.9g carbohydrate; 6.1g protein; 3.4g fibre
tip Granita biscuits are made from flour, wheat flakes, golden syrup, egg and malt, and their crumbly texture makes them perfectly suited to a cheesecake base.

rich chocolate tart

4 egg yolks
2 eggs
¼ cup (55g) caster sugar
⅓ cup (80ml) thickened cream
300g dark eating chocolate, melted
1 teaspoon vanilla extract
pastry
1¼ cups (185g) plain flour
¼ cup (25g) cocoa powder
⅓ cup (55g) icing sugar
150g cold butter, chopped
2 egg yolks
1 teaspoon iced water

1 Make pastry.
2 Grease 24cm-round loose-based flan tin. Roll dough between sheets of baking paper until large enough to line base and side of flan tin. Ease dough into tin, press into side; trim edge. Cover; refrigerate 30 minutes.
3 Preheat oven to 180°C/160°C fan-forced.
4 Line pastry case with baking paper, fill with dried beans or rice; place on oven tray. Bake 15 minutes. Remove paper and beans; bake about 10 minutes or until browned lightly. Cool. Reduce oven to 160°C/140°C fan-forced.
5 Beat egg yolks, eggs and caster sugar in small bowl with electric mixer until thick and creamy; fold in cream, chocolate and extract. Pour chocolate mixture into pastry case.
6 Bake tart about 30 minutes or until filling is set. Cool 10 minutes. Serve tart dusted with a little extra sifted cocoa, if you like.
pastry Blend or process flour, sifted cocoa, sugar and butter until combined. Add egg yolks and the water; process until ingredients just come together. Knead dough on floured surface until smooth. Enclose in plastic wrap; refrigerate 30 minutes.

prep + cook time 1 hour 15 minutes (+ refrigeration) **serves** 10
nutritional count per serving 28.5g total fat (16.6g saturated fat); 1906kJ (456 cal); 44.1g carbohydrate; 7.4g protein; 1.2g fibre

sour cherry chocolate cheesecake

250g plain sweet biscuits
125g butter, melted
680g jar morello cherries
3 x 250g packets cream cheese, softened
3 eggs
¾ cup (180g) sour cream
¼ cup (60ml) lemon juice
1¾ cups (385g) caster sugar
50g dark eating chocolate, melted
¼ cup (25g) cocoa powder

1 Preheat oven to 150°C/130°C fan-forced. Grease 22cm springform tin.
2 Blend or process biscuits until mixture resembles fine breadcrumbs. Add butter; process until combined. Press biscuit mixture evenly over base and 5cm up the side of tin. Place tin on oven tray; refrigerate about 30 minutes or until firm.
3 Meanwhile, drain cherries over small bowl; reserve 1 cup of the juice.
4 Beat cheese, eggs, sour cream, lemon juice and 1 cup of the sugar in large bowl with electric mixer until smooth. Place half of the cheese mixture in medium bowl; stir in chocolate and sifted cocoa.
5 Pour plain and chocolate mixtures alternately into tin; pull a skewer backwards and forwards through mixture for a marbled effect; top with ½ cup of the cherries.
6 Bake cheesecake about 1 hour or until set. Turn oven off; cool in oven with door ajar. Cover; refrigerate several hours or overnight. Stand cheesecake at room temperature 30 minutes before serving.
7 Meanwhile, stir reserved cherry juice and remaining sugar in small saucepan over heat until sugar dissolves; bring to the boil. Boil, uncovered, without stirring, 5 minutes. Stir in remaining cherries. Transfer to medium heatproof jug; cool 10 minutes.
8 Serve cheesecake with cherry sauce.

prep + cook time 1 hour 30 minutes (+ refrigeration & standing)
serves 12
nutritional count per serving 41.5g total fat (25.8g saturated fat); 2847kJ (681 cal); 70.7g carbohydrate; 9.7g protein; 0.8g fibre

roasted pear tart

1 sheet puff pastry
1 egg, beaten lightly
825g can pear halves in natural juice, drained
1 tablespoon pure maple syrup
30g butter, melted

1 Preheat oven to 200°C/180°C fan-forced. Grease oven tray.
2 Cut pastry sheet in half; place pastry halves about 2cm apart on tray, brush with egg.
3 Place three pear halves, cut-side down, on each pastry half; brush pears with combined syrup and butter.
4 Bake tart about 20 minutes or until pastry is puffed and browned lightly.

prep + cook time 30 minutes **serves** 4
nutritional count per serving 17.1g total fat (5.2g saturated fat); 1258kJ (301 cal); 31.4g carbohydrate; 5g protein; 2.6g fibre

roasted nectarine tart

1⅔ cups (250g) plain flour
⅔ cup (110g) icing sugar
125g cold butter, chopped coarsely
1 egg yolk
1 tablespoon iced water,
    approximately
1.6kg small firm nectarines, halved
½ cup (110g) firmly packed
    brown sugar
¼ cup (60ml) orange juice

crème pâtissière
1 cup (250ml) cream
1½ cups (375ml) milk
½ cup (110g) caster sugar
1 vanilla bean, split lengthways
2 eggs
¼ cup (35g) cornflour
90g butter, chopped coarsely

1 Process flour, icing sugar, butter and egg yolk until crumbly. Add enough of the water to process until ingredients come together. Knead dough on floured surface until smooth. Enclose in plastic wrap; refrigerate 30 minutes.
2 Roll pastry between sheets of baking paper until large enough to line base and sides of 19cm x 27cm rectangular loose-based flan tin. Lift pastry into tin; press into base and sides. Place tin on oven tray; refrigerate 30 minutes.
3 Preheat oven to 180°C/160°C fan-forced.
4 Line pastry with baking paper; fill with dried beans or rice. Bake 10 minutes. Remove paper and beans; bake further 10 minutes or until browned lightly. Cool.
5 Increase oven to 220°C/200°C fan-forced.
6 Place nectarines in large baking dish; sprinkle with brown sugar and juice. Roast, uncovered, about 20 minutes or until nectarines are soft.
7 Meanwhile, make crème pâtissière.
8 Spoon crème pâtissière into pastry case; refrigerate tart 30 minutes or until firm. Top with nectarines.
crème pâtissière Bring cream, milk, sugar and vanilla bean to the boil in medium saucepan. Whisk eggs in medium bowl; whisk in sifted cornflour. Gradually whisk in hot milk mixture. Strain mixture back into same pan; stir over heat until mixture boils and thickens. Remove from heat; whisk in butter. Cover surface of custard with plastic wrap; cool.

prep + cook time 1 hour (+ refrigeration) **serves** 8
nutritional count per serving 40.3g total fat (25.4g saturated fat); 3022kJ (723 cal); 81.7g carbohydrate; 8.6g protein; 5.2g fibre

fruit mince slice

¾ cup (110g) plain flour
½ cup (75g) self-raising flour
2 tablespoons caster sugar
100g cold butter, chopped coarsely
1 egg yolk
1 tablespoon milk
410g jar fruit mince
2 large apples (400g), peeled, grated coarsely
1 sheet puff pastry
1 egg yolk, extra

1 Grease 19cm x 29cm lamington pan; line base and long sides with baking paper, extending paper 5cm over sides.
2 Sift flours and sugar into large bowl; rub in butter then stir in egg yolk and milk. Turn dough onto floured surface, knead gently until smooth. Cover; refrigerate 30 minutes.
3 Preheat oven to 200°C/180°C fan-forced.
4 Roll dough between sheets of baking paper until large enough to cover base of pan; press into pan. Spread combined fruit mince and apple over dough.
5 Cut sheet puff pastry into 2cm-wide strips; place strips over filling in a lattice pattern. Brush pastry with a little extra egg yolk.
6 Bake slice about 30 minutes. Cool in pan before cutting.

prep + cook time 1 hour (+ refrigeration) **serves** 18
nutritional count per serving 8.1g total fat (3.6g saturated fat); 786kJ (188 cal); 26.3g carbohydrate; 2.3g protein; 1.5g fibre

rich chocolate coconut tart

1 cup (90g) desiccated coconut
1 egg white, beaten lightly
¼ cup (55g) caster sugar
300ml cream
300g dark eating chocolate, chopped finely
4 egg yolks
2 teaspoons coffee-flavoured liqueur

1 Preheat oven to 150°C/130°C fan-forced. Insert base of 20cm non-stick springform tin upside down in tin to give a flat base; grease tin.
2 Combine coconut, egg white and sugar; press mixture evenly over base and 4cm up side of tin.
3 Bake base about 40 minutes or until golden. Cool.
4 Heat cream until almost boiling; stir in chocolate until smooth. Cool slightly. Whisk egg yolks and liqueur into chocolate mixture; strain. Pour chocolate mixture into coconut shell.
5 Refrigerate tart 6 hours or until set. Cut into thin wedges to serve.

prep + cook time 50 minutes (+ refrigeration) **serves** 12
nutritional count per serving 24.6g total fat (16.3g saturated fat); 1329kJ (318 cal); 21.6g carbohydrate; 3.4g protein; 1.4g fibre

chocolate raspberry tart

¾ cup (240g) raspberry jam
200g dark eating chocolate, chopped finely
25g unsalted butter, melted
⅔ cup (160ml) cream, warmed
120g raspberries
sweet pastry
1¼ cups (185g) plain flour
½ cup (80g) icing sugar
125g cold unsalted butter, chopped coarsely
¼ cup (60ml) iced water, approximately

1 Make sweet pastry.
2 Grease 12.5cm x 35cm (or 24cm-round) loose-based flan tin. Roll pastry between sheets of baking paper until large enough to line tin. Ease pastry into tin, press into base and side; trim edge, prick base with fork. Cover; refrigerate 30 minutes.
3 Preheat oven to 200°C/180°C fan-forced.
4 Place tin on oven tray; line pastry with baking paper, fill with dried beans or uncooked rice. Bake 15 minutes; remove paper and beans. Bake about 10 minutes. Spread jam over pastry base; bake further 2 minutes. Cool.
5 Whisk chocolate, butter and cream in medium bowl until smooth. Pour chocolate mixture into pastry case; refrigerate 2 hours. Top tart with raspberries.
sweet pastry Process flour, icing sugar and butter until crumbly; add enough of the water to make ingredients come together. Knead dough gently on floured surface until smooth. Enclose in plastic wrap; refrigerate 30 minutes.

prep + cook time 40 minutes (+ refrigeration) **serves** 12
nutritional count per serving 21g total fat (13.4g saturated fat); 1559kJ (373 cal); 42.4g carbohydrate; 3g protein; 1.6g fibre

lime curd tart

3 eggs
4 egg yolks
2 teaspoons finely grated lime rind
½ cup (125ml) lime juice
1 cup (220g) caster sugar
200g unsalted butter, chopped
1 cup (50g) flaked coconut
sweet pastry
1¼ cups (185g) plain flour
½ cup (80g) icing sugar
¼ cup (20g) desiccated coconut
125g cold unsalted butter
¼ cup (60ml) iced water, approximately

1 Make sweet pastry.
2 Grease 24cm-round loose-based flan tin. Roll pastry between sheets of baking paper until large enough to line tin. Ease pastry into tin, press into base and side; trim edge, prick base with fork. Enclose in plastic wrap; refrigerate 30 minutes.
3 Preheat oven to 200°C/180°C fan-forced.
4 Place tin on oven tray; line pastry with baking paper, fill with dried beans or rice. Bake 15 minutes; remove paper and beans. Bake about 10 minutes; cool.
5 Meanwhile, stir whole eggs, egg yolks, rind, juice, sugar and butter in medium saucepan over medium heat, without boiling, about 15 minutes or until mixture coats the back of a spoon. Strain lime curd through sieve into medium bowl; stand 10 minutes.
6 Pour curd into pastry case; refrigerate 2 hours. Serve tart sprinkled with coconut.
sweet pastry Process flour, sugar, coconut and butter until crumbly; add enough of the water to make ingredients come together. Knead dough gently on floured surface until smooth. Enclose in plastic wrap; refrigerate 30 minutes.

prep + cook time 40 minutes (+ refrigeration) **serves** 10
nutritional count per serving 35.4g total fat (22.9g saturated fat); 2178kJ (521 cal); 44.2g carbohydrate; 6g protein; 1.8g fibre

lemon tart

1 ¼ cups (185g) plain flour
¼ cup (40g) icing sugar
¼ cup (30g) ground almonds
125g cold butter, chopped
1 egg yolk

lemon filling
1 tablespoon finely grated
  lemon rind
½ cup (125ml) lemon juice
5 eggs
¾ cup (165g) caster sugar
1 cup (250ml) thickened cream

1 Blend or process flour, icing sugar, ground nuts and butter until combined. Add egg yolk, process until ingredients just come together. Knead dough on floured surface until smooth. Enclose in plastic wrap, refrigerate 30 minutes.

2 Roll pastry between sheets of baking paper until large enough to line 24cm-round loose-based flan tin. Ease dough into tin; trim edge. Cover; refrigerate 30 minutes.

3 Meanwhile, preheat oven to 200°C/180°C fan-forced.

4 Place tin on oven tray. Line pastry case with baking paper, fill with dried beans or rice. Bake 15 minutes. Remove paper and beans; bake about 10 minutes or until browned lightly.

5 Meanwhile, make lemon filling.

6 Reduce oven to 180°C/160°C fan-forced.

7 Pour lemon filling into pastry case; bake tart about 30 minutes or until filling has set slightly. Cool. Refrigerate until cold.

8 Serve tart dusted with sifted icing sugar, if you like.

lemon filling Whisk ingredients in medium bowl; stand 5 minutes.

prep + cook time 1 hour 15 minutes (+ refrigeration & standing)
serves 8
nutritional count per serving 31.1g total fat (17.6g saturated fat); 2044kJ (489 cal); 44.1g carbohydrate; 9.2g protein; 1.3g fibre
tip You need about 3 medium lemons (420g) for this tart.

low-fat chocolate and ricotta tart

¼ cup (35g) white
  self-raising flour
¼ cup (40g) wholemeal
  self-raising flour
2 tablespoons caster sugar
2 teaspoons cocoa powder
30g low-fat margarine
2 teaspoons water
1 egg yolk

ricotta filling
150g low-fat ricotta cheese
1 egg
1 egg yolk
¼ cup (70g) low-fat plain yogurt
¼ cup (55g) caster sugar
2 teaspoons plain flour
2 tablespoons dark choc chips
2 teaspoons coffee-flavoured
  liqueur

1 Process flours, sugar, sifted cocoa and spread until crumbly; add the water and egg yolk, process until ingredients just cling together. Knead dough gently on floured surface until smooth. Enclose in plastic wrap; refrigerate 30 minutes.

2 Preheat oven to 200°C/180°C fan-forced.

3 Grease 18cm-round loose-based flan tin. Press pastry into tin; place on oven tray. Line pastry with baking paper; fill with dried beans or rice. Bake 10 minutes; remove beans and paper. Bake further 5 minutes or until pastry is lightly browned; cool.

4 Reduce oven to 180°C/160°C fan-forced.

5 Make ricotta filling; pour into cooled pastry case.

6 Bake tart about 20 minutes; cool. Refrigerate until firm.

ricotta filling Beat ricotta, egg, egg yolk, yogurt, sugar and flour in medium bowl with electric mixer until smooth. Stir in choc bits and liqueur.

prep + cook time 45 minutes (+ refrigeration & standing) **serves** 8
nutritional count per serving 6.4g total fat (2.6g saturated fat); 702kJ (168 cal); 21.8g carbohydrate; 5.5g protein; 0.8g fibre

quince tarte tartin

4 medium quinces (1.2kg)
1 cup (220g) caster sugar
1 litre (4 cups) water
¼ cup (60ml) orange juice
1 teaspoon finely grated
  orange rind
40g butter

pastry
1 cup (150g) plain flour
¼ cup (40g) icing sugar
100g butter, chopped
1 egg yolk
1 tablespoon cold water,
  approximately

1 Peel and core quinces; quarter lengthways.
2 Place quince in large saucepan with sugar, the water, juice and rind; bring to the boil. Reduce heat; simmer, covered, about 2½ hours or until quince is rosy in colour. Using slotted spoon, remove quinces from syrup; bring syrup to the boil. Boil, uncovered, until syrup reduces to ¾ cup. Stir in butter.
3 Meanwhile, make pastry.
4 Preheat oven to 200°C/180°C fan-forced. Line base of deep 22cm-round cake pan with baking paper.
5 Place quince, rounded-sides down, in pan; pour syrup over quince.
6 Roll pastry between sheets of baking paper until large enough to line base of pan. Lift pastry into pan, tucking pastry down side of pan.
7 Bake tart about 30 minutes or until pastry is browned lightly. Cool in pan 5 minutes; turn tart onto serving plate.
pastry Blend or process flour, sugar and butter until crumbly. Add egg yolk and enough of the water to make the ingredients just come together. Shape dough into ball, enclose in plastic wrap; refrigerate 30 minutes.

prep + cook time 3 hours 20 minutes (+ refrigeration) **serves** 6
nutritional count per serving 20.7g total fat (12.9g saturated fat); 2098kJ (502 cal); 77.5g carbohydrate; 4.1g protein; 11.3g fibre

new york cheesecake

250g plain sweet biscuits
125g butter, melted
750g cream cheese, softened
2 teaspoons finely grated orange rind
1 teaspoon finely grated lemon rind
1 cup (220g) caster sugar
3 eggs
¾ cup (180g) sour cream
¼ cup (60ml) lemon juice
sour cream topping
1 cup (240g) sour cream
2 tablespoons caster sugar
2 teaspoons lemon juice

1 Process biscuits until fine. Add butter, process until combined.
Press mixture over base and side of 24cm springform tin. Place tin on
oven tray; refrigerate 30 minutes.
2 Preheat oven to 180°C/160°C fan-forced.
3 Beat cream cheese, rinds and sugar in medium bowl with electric mixer
until smooth. Beat in eggs, one at a time, then sour cream and juice.
4 Pour filling into tin; bake 1¼ hours. Remove from oven; cool 15 minutes.
5 Make sour cream topping; spread over cheesecake.
6 Bake cheesecake 20 minutes; cool in oven with door ajar. Refrigerate
cheesecake 3 hours or overnight.
sour cream topping Combine ingredients in small bowl.

prep + cook time 2 hours 30 minutes (+ refrigeration & cooling)
serves 12
nutritional count per serving 47.8g total fat (30.1g saturated fat);
2587kJ (619 cal); 39g carbohydrate; 9.2g protein; 0.4g fibre

lemon cheesecake

250g packet plain sweet biscuits
125g butter, melted
filling
250g packet cream cheese, softened
400g can sweetened condensed milk
2 teaspoons grated lemon rind
⅓ cup (80ml) lemon juice
1 teaspoon gelatine
1 tablespoon water

1 Grease 20cm springform tin.
2 Blend or process biscuits until crushed finely; stir in butter. Using a flat-bottomed glass, press mixture evenly over base and side of tin. Refrigerate 30 minutes or until firm.
3 Make filling.
4 Pour filling into crumb crust; refrigerate several hours or until set. Serve with whipped cream, if you like.
filling Beat cream cheese in small bowl with electric mixer until smooth. Beat in condensed milk, rind and juice until smooth. Sprinkle gelatine over the water in small heatproof jug; stand jug in small saucepan of simmering water, stirring, until gelatine is dissolved. Stir gelatine mixture into lemon mixture.

prep time 15 minutes (+ standing) **serves** 8
nutritional count per serving 32.9g total fat (20.6g saturated fat); 2211kJ (529 cal); 50.9g carbohydrate; 9.3g protein; 0.7g fibre

gluten-free berry tarts

75g butter, softened
½ teaspoon vanilla extract
⅓ cup (75g) caster sugar
1 egg
¾ cup (90g) ground almond
1 tablespoon (corn) cornflour
150g fresh blueberries and raspberries
1 tablespoon pure icing sugar

1 Preheat oven to 180°C/160°C fan-forced. Grease six 5.5cm x 10.5cm loose-based fluted flan tins; place on oven tray.
2 Beat butter, extract and caster sugar in small bowl with electric mixer until light and fluffy. Add egg; beat until combined. Stir in ground nuts and cornflour. Spoon mixture into tins; smooth surface, sprinkle with berries.
3 Bake tarts about 30 minutes. Stand in tins 10 minutes; turn carefully, top-side up, onto baking-paper-covered wire rack.
4 Serve tarts warm or cold, dusted with sifted icing sugar.

prep + cook time 45 minutes **makes** 6
nutritional count per tart 19.5g total fat (7.6g saturated fat); 1133kJ (271 cal); 18.8g carbohydrate; 4.4g protein; 2.2g fibre
tip This recipe is also wheat-free and yeast-free.

berry frangipane tart

1 sheet sweet puff pastry
300g frozen mixed berries
frangipane
80g butter, softened
½ teaspoon vanilla extract
⅓ cup (75g) caster sugar
2 egg yolks
1 tablespoon plain flour
1 cup (120g) ground almonds

1 Preheat oven to 220°C/200°C fan-forced. Grease 20cm x 30cm lamington pan.
2 Roll pastry until large enough to cover base and sides of pan. Line pan with pastry, press into sides. Prick pastry all over with fork; freeze 5 minutes.
3 Place another lamington pan on top of pastry; bake 5 minutes. Remove top pan; bake about 5 minutes or until pastry is browned lightly. Cool 5 minutes. Reduce oven to 180°C/160°C fan-forced.
4 Meanwhile, make frangipane.
5 Spread frangipane over pastry base. Sprinkle with berries, press into frangipane. Bake about 30 minutes or until browned lightly.
frangipane Beat butter, extract, sugar and egg yolks in small bowl with electric mixer until light and fluffy. Stir in flour and ground almonds.

prep + cook time 45 minutes **serves** 6
nutritional count per serving 30.2g total fat (11.9g saturated fat); 1722kJ (412 cal); 26.4g carbohydrate; 7.7g protein; 3.3g fibre

apple pie slice

1 cup (150g) self-raising flour
½ cup (75g) plain flour
80g cold butter, chopped coarsely
¼ cup (55g) caster sugar
1 egg, beaten lightly
¼ cup (60ml) milk, approximately
1 tablespoon milk, extra
1 tablespoon caster sugar, extra

apple filling
6 medium apples (900g), peeled, cored, cut into 1cm pieces
¼ cup (55g) caster sugar
¼ cup (60ml) water
¾ cup (120g) sultanas
1 teaspoon mixed spice
2 teaspoons finely grated lemon rind

1 Make apple filling.
2 Grease 20cm x 30cm lamington pan; line base with baking paper, extending paper 5cm over long sides.
3 Sift flours into medium bowl, rub in butter. Stir in sugar, egg and enough milk to make a firm dough. Knead dough on floured surface until smooth. Enclose in plastic wrap; refrigerate 30 minutes.
4 Preheat oven to 200°C/180°C fan-forced.
5 Divide dough in half. Roll one half large enough to cover base of pan; press firmly into pan. Spread apple filling over dough. Roll remaining dough large enough to cover filling and place over the top. Brush with extra milk; sprinkle with extra sugar.
6 Bake slice about 25 minutes. Stand slice in pan 5 minutes.

apple filling Cook apple, sugar and the water in large saucepan, uncovered, stirring occasionally, about 10 minutes or until apple softens. Remove from heat; stir in sultanas, spice and rind. Cool.

prep + cook time 45 minutes (+ refrigeration) **serves** 8
nutritional count per serving 9.7g total fat (5.9g saturated fat);
1463kJ (350 cal); 58.6g carbohydrate; 4.8g protein; 3.4g fibre

prune and custard tart

1½ cups (250g) seeded prunes
2 tablespoons brandy
300ml cream
3 eggs
⅔ cup (150g) caster sugar
1 teaspoon vanilla extract

pastry
1¼ cups (175g) plain flour
⅓ cup (55g) icing sugar
¼ cup (30g) ground almonds
125g cold butter, chopped coarsely
1 egg yolk
1 tablespoon iced water,
 approximately

1 Make pastry.
2 Grease 26cm-round loose-based flan tin. Roll pastry between sheets of baking paper until large enough to line tin. Lift pastry into tin, ease into base and side; trim edge, prick base all over with fork. Refrigerate 20 minutes.
3 Preheat oven to 200°C/180°C fan-forced.
4 Place tin on oven tray. Line pastry with baking paper; fill with dried beans or rice. Bake 10 minutes. Remove paper and beans; bake about 5 minutes. Cool. Reduce oven to 150°C/130°C fan-forced.
5 Blend or process prunes and brandy until combined; spread into pastry cases.
6 Bring cream to the boil in small saucepan; remove from heat. Whisk eggs, sugar and extract in small bowl; whisk in hot cream. Pour custard mixture into pastry case.
7 Bake tart about 20 minutes or until custard sets. Stand 10 minutes before serving.
pastry Process flour, sugar, ground nuts and butter until crumbly. Add egg yolk and enough of the water to process until ingredients come together. Enclose in plastic wrap; refrigerate 30 minutes.

prep + cook time 50 minutes (+ refrigeration) **serves** 8
nutritional count per serving 34.3g total fat (20.3g saturated fat); 2383kJ (570 cal); 57.4g carbohydrate; 7.7g protein; 3.7g fibre

almond jalousie

375g packet puff pastry
1 tablespoon apricot jam
1 egg white
2 teaspoons caster sugar
almond filling
30g butter
1 cup (80g) flaked almonds
2 tablespoons caster sugar
1 teaspoon vanilla extract
2 egg yolks
2 teaspoons plain flour

1 Make almond filling.
2 Preheat oven to 220°C/200°C fan-forced.
3 Cut pastry in half, roll one half into neatly trimmed 12cm x 25cm rectangle; place on oven tray. Spread warmed sieved jam over centre. Place almond filling on pastry leaving a 2cm border around the edge.
4 Roll remaining pastry into a neatly trimmed 13cm x 27cm rectangle; fold in half lengthways. Brush pastry on both sides with egg white. Cut through folded edge of pastry at 2cm intervals leaving a 2cm border down long side of pastry strip.
5 Brush around edge of pastry strip on oven tray with egg white. Carefully unfold cut pastry strip, place over almond filling. Press edges of pastry together using thumb and back of knife to make decorative edge. Brush evenly with egg white, sprinkle with sugar. Bake 5 minutes.
6 Reduce oven to 200°C/180°C fan-forced; bake further 10 minutes or until golden brown.
almond filling Melt butter in small saucepan; cook almonds, stirring constantly, over heat until browned lightly. Process almond mixture with remaining ingredients until smooth.

prep + cook time 35 minutes (+ standing) **serves** 8
nutritional count per serving 20.3g total fat (3.5g saturated fat); 1292kJ (309 cal); 26g carbohydrate; 5.8g protein; 1.6g fibre
tip Jalousie is best made on the day of serving. Serve with whipped cream if you like.

anise and triple nut tart

3 cups (450g) plain flour
2 tablespoons caster sugar
150g cold butter, chopped
1 egg, beaten lightly
¼ cup (60ml) iced water,
   approximately
¾ cup (180ml) thickened cream
⅓ cup (75g) caster sugar, extra
¼ cup (55g) firmly packed
   brown sugar

¼ cup (60ml) honey
½ teaspoon finely chopped
   star anise
⅓ cup (40g) coarsely chopped
   walnuts
⅓ cup (45g) slivered almonds
⅓ cup (50g) pine nuts
⅓ cup (65g) chopped dried figs

1 Sift flour and caster sugar into bowl, rub in butter. Add egg and enough water to make ingredients cling together. Press dough into a ball, knead on floured surface until smooth. Divide dough in half, wrap in plastic; refrigerate 30 minutes.

2 Roll one half of the pastry between sheets of baking paper until large enough to fit 24cm round loose-base flan tin. Ease pastry into side, trim edge; reserve trimmings. Prick base with fork; refrigerate 30 minutes.

3 Preheat oven to 200°C/180°C fan-forced.

4 Line pastry case with baking paper, fill with dried beans or rice; place on oven tray. Bake 10 minutes. Remove paper and beans; bake further 10 minutes or until lightly browned. Cool.

5 Roll remaining pastry (including scraps) between sheets of baking paper into 28cm square, cut into 1cm strips. Interweave strips on sheet of baking paper to form lattice large enough to cover tart; cover, refrigerate.

6 Stir cream, extra sugar, brown sugar, honey and star anise in heavy based saucepan, over low heat, without boiling, until sugar dissolves. Boil about 7 minutes, without stirring, or until mixture turns golden brown. Cool 10 minutes; gently stir in nuts and figs.

7 Reduce oven to 180°C/160°C fan-forced.

8 Spread filling into pastry case, gently turn lattice off paper onto tart; trim edge. Bake about 25 minutes or until browned. Serve tart with whipped cream, if you like.

prep + cook time 1 hour (+ refrigeration) **serves** 8
nutritional count per serving 36.2g total fat (16.7g saturated fat); 2801kJ (670 cal); 75.5g carbohydrate; 10.6g protein; 4.4g fibre

apricot cheesecake

125g butter, melted
2 cups (200g) plain sweet biscuit crumbs
150g dried apricots
2 tablespoons water
2 tablespoons lemon juice
125g packet cream cheese, softened
½ cup (110g) caster sugar
3 eggs
300ml thickened cream

1 Combine butter and crumbs in medium bowl; press evenly over base and side of 23m flan tin. Refrigerate 30 minutes.
2 Place apricots, the water and half of the juice in small saucepan, cover, bring to the boil. Reduce heat; simmer, covered, about 15 minutes or until soft. Cool slightly. Blend or process apricot mixture until pulpy.
3 Preheat oven to 160°C/140°C fan-forced.
4 Beat cheese, sugar and remaining juice in small bowl with electric mixer until smooth. Beat in eggs one at a time. Beat in cream until combined.
5 Pour apricot mixture into crumb crust, then pour in cheese mixture; swirl through with knife for marbled effect.
6 Bake cheesecake about 1 hour or until set. Cool in oven with door ajar; refrigerate before serving.

prep + cook time 1 hour 30 minutes (+ refrigeration & standing)
serves 10
nutritional count per serving 32.1g total fat (19.8 g saturated fat); 1827kJ (437 cal); 31.1g carbohydrate; 5.6g protein; 1.7g fibre

bakewell tart

100g butter, softened
2 tablespoons caster sugar
1 egg yolk
1 cup (150g) plain flour
½ cup (60g) ground almonds
1½ tablespoons raspberry jam
2 tablespoons apricot jam

filling
125g butter, softened
½ cup (110g) caster sugar
2 eggs
¾ cup (90g) ground almonds
2 tablespoons rice flour
½ teaspoon grated lemon rind
lemon icing
⅓ cup (55g) icing sugar
2 teaspoons lemon juice

1 Beat butter, sugar and egg yolk in small bowl with electric mixer until combined. Stir in sifted flour and ground almonds in two batches. Knead dough on floured surface until smooth; cover, refrigerate 30 minutes.
2 Preheat oven to 200°C/180°C fan-forced.
3 Roll dough between sheets of baking paper until large enough to line 24cm flan tin. Lift pastry into tin, ease into base and side; trim edge.
4 Make filling.
5 Spread base of pastry with raspberry jam; spread filling over jam. Place tart on oven tray; bake 25 minutes or until lightly browned.
6 Heat apricot jam in small saucepan; strain. Brush top of hot tart with hot jam; cool.
7 Make lemon icing; pipe or drizzle icing over cool tart.
filling Beat butter and sugar in small bowl with electric mixer until light and fluffy. Beat in eggs one at a time. Stir in almonds, rice flour and rind.
lemon icing Sift icing sugar into small bowl, stir in juice until smooth.

prep + cook time 45 minutes **serves** 8
nutritional count per serving 35.8g total fat (16.6g saturated fat); 2303kJ (551 cal); 50.2g carbohydrate; 8.4g protein; 2.6g fibre

nectarine and macadamia tart

1¼ cups (185g) plain flour
2 tablespoons caster sugar
90g cold butter, chopped
1 egg yolk
½ teaspoon vanilla extract
2 teaspoons cold water,
    approximately
3 medium nectarines (500g),
    cut into eighths

macadamia filling
¾ cup (110g) macadamias
¼ cup (35g) plain flour
75g butter
⅓ cup (75g) firmly packed
    brown sugar
1 egg
1 egg yolk
2 tablespoons maple syrup

1 Blend or process flour, sugar and butter until combined. Add egg yolk, extract and enough of the water to make ingredients just come together. Knead dough on floured surface until smooth. Enclose in plastic wrap; refrigerate 30 minutes.

2 Roll dough between sheets of baking paper until large enough to line base and side of 24cm-round, loose-based flan tin. Ease dough into tin; trim edge. Place tin on oven tray; cover, refrigerate 30 minutes.

3 Meanwhile, preheat oven to 180°C/160°C fan-forced.

4 Line pastry case with baking paper; fill with dried beans or rice. Bake 20 minutes; remove paper and beans. Bake about 5 minutes or until browned lightly.

5 Meanwhile, make macadamia filling.

6 Spread filling into pastry case; arrange nectarine segments over filling.

7 Bake tart about 35 minutes or until golden brown and firm to touch. Cool.

macadamia filling Process macadamias and 2 tablespoons of the flour until fine. Beat butter and sugar in small bowl with electric mixer until pale. Beat in egg and egg yolk until combined; fold in syrup, macadamia mixture and remaining flour.

prep + cook time 1 hour 15 minutes (+ refrigeration) **serves** 8
nutritional count per serving 29.7g total fat (13.2g saturated fat);
1940kJ (464 cal); 42.8g carbohydrate; 6.4g protein; 3g fibre

butterscotch pie

1½ cups (225g) plain flour
125g cold butter, chopped
1 egg yolk
3 teaspoons iced water, approximately
2 x 400g can sweetened condensed milk
⅓ cup (80ml) golden syrup
125g butter, chopped, extra
¾ cup (180ml) cream
80g packaged butterscotch, crushed

1 Sift flour into bowl, rub in butter (or process flour and butter until mixture resembles breadcrumbs). Add egg yolk and enough water to make ingredients cling together (or process until ingredients just come together). Press dough into a ball, knead gently on floured surface until smooth. Wrap in plastic; refrigerate 30 minutes.
2 Grease 24cm round loose-base flan tin. Roll pastry between sheets of baking paper until large enough to line tin. Lift pastry into tin, ease into side; trim edge. Prick pastry base with fork; refrigerate 30 minutes.
3 Preheat oven to 200°C/180°C fan-forced.
4 Line pastry with baking paper, fill with dried beans or rice; place on oven tray. Bake 10 minutes. Remove paper and beans; bake further 10 minutes or until browned. Cool.
5 Cook condensed milk, golden syrup and extra butter in heavy-based saucepan, stirring, about 20 minutes or until mixture is dark golden brown. Stand mixture 10 minutes, stir in cream; strain; cover; cool.
6 Spread mixture into pastry case, refrigerate until firm. Decorate with crushed butterscotch. Serve with whipped cream, if you like.

prep + cook time 1 hour (+ refrigeration) **serves** 8
nutritional count per serving 46.7g total fat (30.5g saturated fat); 3461kJ (828 cal); 93.9g carbohydrate; 12.6g protein; 1.2g fibre

blueberry and fillo pastry stacks

4 sheets fillo pastry
cooking-oil spray
125g packaged light cream cheese
½ cup (125ml) light cream
2 teaspoons finely grated orange rind
2 tablespoons icing sugar
blueberry sauce
300g blueberries
¼ cup (55g) caster sugar
2 tablespoons orange juice
1 teaspoon cornflour

1 Preheat oven to 200°C/180°C fan-forced. Grease oven trays.
2 Spray one fillo sheet with oil; layer with another fillo sheet. Halve fillo stack lengthways; cut each half into thirds to form six fillo squares. Repeat process with remaining fillo sheets. Place 12 fillo squares onto trays; spray with oil.
3 Bake fillo squares about 5 minutes or until browned lightly; cool 10 minutes.
4 Meanwhile, make blueberry sauce.
5 Beat cheese, cream, rind and half of the sugar in small bowl with electric mixer until smooth.
6 Place one fillo square on each serving plate; spoon half of the cheese mixture and half of the blueberry sauce over squares. Repeat layering process, finishing with fillo squares; dust with remaining sifted icing sugar.
blueberry sauce Cook blueberries, sugar and half of the juice in small saucepan, stirring, until sugar dissolves. Stir in blended cornflour and remaining juice; cook, stirring, until mixture boils and thickens slightly. Remove from heat; cool 10 minutes.

prep + cook time 30 minutes **serves** 4
nutritional count per serving 14.5g total fat (9g saturated fat); 1321kJ (316 cal); 40.7g carbohydrate; 5.8g protein; 1.9g fibre

almond pear flan

1¼ cups (185g) plain flour
90g butter
¼ cup (55g) caster sugar
2 egg yolks
3 firm ripe medium pears (690g), peeled, cored, quartered
2 tablespoons apricot jam, warmed, strained
almond filling
125g butter, softened
⅓ cup (75g) caster sugar
2 eggs
1 cup (120g) ground almonds
1 tablespoon plain flour

1 Blend or process flour, butter, sugar and egg yolks until just combined. Knead dough on floured surface until smooth. Enclose in plastic wrap; refrigerate 30 minutes.
2 Meanwhile, make almond filling.
3 Preheat oven to 180°C/160°C fan-forced. Grease 23cm-round loose-based flan tin.
4 Roll dough between sheets of baking paper; press dough evenly into base and side of tin. Spread filling into pastry case; arrange pears over filling.
5 Bake flan about 45 minutes. Brush top of flan with jam.
almond filling Beat butter and sugar in small bowl with electric mixer until just combined. Beat in eggs, one at a time. Fold in ground almonds and flour.

prep + cook time 1 hour (+ standing) **serves** 10
nutritional count per serving 26.7g total fat (12.7g saturated fat); 1751kJ (419 cal); 38.4g carbohydrate; 6.9g protein; 2.8g fibre

impossible pie

½ cup (75g) plain flour
1 cup (220g) caster sugar
¾ cup (60g) desiccated coconut
4 eggs
1 teaspoon vanilla extract
125g butter, melted
½ cup (40g) flaked almonds
2 cups (500ml) milk

1 Preheat oven to 180°C/160°C fan-forced. Grease deep 24cm pie dish.
2 Combine sifted flour, sugar, coconut, eggs, extract, butter and half the nuts in large bowl; gradually add milk, stirring, until combined. Pour mixture into dish.
3 Bake pie 35 minutes. Remove pie from oven, sprinkle top with remaining nuts; bake further 10 minutes. Serve with cream, if you like.

prep + cook time 55 minutes **serves** 8
nutritional count per serving 26g total fat (15.5g saturated fat); 1735kJ (415 cal); 38.2g carbohydrate; 8.5g protein; 1.9g fibre

lime chiffon pie

250g plain sweet biscuits
125g butter, melted
4 eggs, separated
⅓ cup (75g) caster sugar
3 teaspoons gelatine
2 teaspoons finely grated lime rind
⅓ cup (80ml) lime juice
⅓ cup (80ml) water
⅓ cup (75g) caster sugar, extra

1 Grease deep 23cm pie dish.
2 Process biscuits until fine; add butter, process until combined. Press mixture firmly over base and side of dish; refrigerate 30 minutes.
3 Combine egg yolks, sugar, gelatine, rind, juice and the water in medium heatproof bowl. Whisk over medium saucepan of simmering water until mixture thickens slightly. Remove from heat; pour mixture into large bowl. Cover; cool.
4 Beat egg whites in small bowl with electric mixer until soft peaks form; gradually add extra sugar, beating until sugar dissolves. Fold meringue into filling mixture, in two batches.
5 Spread filling into crumb crust; refrigerate 3 hours.

prep + cook time 35 minutes (+ refrigeration & standing) **serves** 6
nutritional count per serving 27.8g total fat (15.8g saturated fat); 2094kJ (501 cal); 54.8g carbohydrate; 9.3g protein; 0.9g fibre

pecan pie

1 cup (120g) pecans,
   chopped coarsely
2 tablespoons cornflour
1 cup (220g) firmly packed
   brown sugar
60g butter, melted
2 tablespoons cream
1 teaspoon vanilla extract
3 eggs
⅓ cup (40g) pecans, extra
2 tablespoons apricot jam,
   warmed, sieved

pastry
1¼ cups (185g) plain flour
⅓ cup (55g) icing sugar
125g cold butter, chopped
1 egg yolk
1 teaspoon water

1 Make pastry.

2 Grease 24cm-round loose-based flan tin. Roll pastry between sheets of baking paper until large enough to line tin. Ease pastry into tin, press into base and side; trim edge. Cover; refrigerate 30 minutes.

3 Preheat oven to 180°C/160°C fan-forced.

4 Place tin on oven tray. Line pastry case with baking paper; fill with dried beans or rice. Bake 10 minutes; remove paper and beans. Bake about 5 minutes; cool.

5 Reduce oven to 160°C/140°C fan-forced.

6 Combine chopped nuts and cornflour in medium bowl. Stir in sugar, butter, cream, extract and eggs until combined. Pour mixture into shell, sprinkle with extra nuts.

7 Bake pie about 45 minutes; cool. Brush pie with jam.

pastry Process flour, icing sugar and butter until crumbly. Add egg yolk and the water; process until ingredients just come together. Knead dough on floured surface until smooth. Enclose in plastic wrap; refrigerate 30 minutes.

prep + cook time 1 hour 15 minutes (+ refrigeration) **serves** 10
nutritional count per serving 30.9g total fat (12.6g saturated fat); 2023kJ (484 cal); 46.5g carbohydrate; 6.3g protein; 2.1g fibre

apple galette

500g packet puff pastry roll
4 large apples (800g), cored
2 tablespoons lemon juice
1 tablespoon caster sugar
60g butter, chopped
2 tablespoons apricot jam, warmed, sieved

1 Preheat oven to 240°C/220°C fan-forced.
2 Cut a 35cm length from puff pastry roll; place on oven tray. Turn edges in about 2cm, press lightly.
3 Thinly slice whole apples, toss in juice; place on pastry. Sprinkle with sugar, dot with half the butter.
4 Place galette in oven; reduce to 200°C/180°C fan-forced, bake 20 minutes. Dot galette with remaining butter; bake further 25 minutes or until browned. Brush hot galette with jam. Serve warm or cold with whipped cream, if you like.

prep + cook time 1 hour **serves** 6
nutritional count per serving 26.9g total fat (6.7g saturated fat); 1944kJ (465 cal); 50g carbohydrate; 5g protein; 3.3g fibre
tip We used a combination of granny smith and red-skinned apples in this recipe.

pear, brandy and almond tart

3 medium firm pears (540g),
  peeled, cored, halved
2 tablespoons lemon juice
¼ cup (60ml) brandy
1½ cups (225g) plain flour
⅔ cup (80g) ground almonds
⅓ cup (75g) caster sugar
185g cold unsalted butter
2 egg yolks
¾ cup (180ml) thickened cream

almond filling
125g soft butter
¼ teaspoon almond essence
½ cup (110g) caster sugar
2 eggs
1 tablespoon plain flour
1 cup (125g) ground almonds

1 Preheat oven to 180°C/160°C fan-forced.

2 Brush pears with juice, place in shallow ovenproof dish; sprinkle with 2 tablespoons of the brandy. Bake, covered, about 20 minutes or until just tender. Cool. Strain pears, reserve liquid.

3 Sift flour into bowl, add ground almonds and sugar, rub in butter. Add egg yolks, mix until ingredients cling together. Press dough into a ball, wrap in plastic; refrigerate 1 hour.

4 Roll two-thirds of the pastry between sheets of baking paper until large enough to line 3.5cm deep x 24cm round loose-base flan tin. Ease pastry into tin, press base and side; trim edge. Prick with fork; refrigerate 30 minutes.

5 Meanwhile, make almond filling.

6 Spread almond filling over base of pastry case, place pears around edge. Roll remaining pastry between sheets of baking paper until large enough to cover tart; gently cover pears with pastry, trim edge. Brush with water, sprinkle with a little extra sugar.

7 Bake tart 1 hour or until browned. Stand 15 minutes before serving.

8 Meanwhile, beat cream until soft peaks form; fold in reserved liquid and remaining brandy.

9 Serve tart, dusted with extra icing sugar if you like, with brandy cream.

almond filling Beat butter, essence and sugar in small bowl with electric mixer until thick and creamy. Beat in eggs, one at a time; fold in flour and ground almonds.

prep + cook time 1 hour 20 minutes (+ refrigeration & standing) **serves** 8
nutritional count per serving 57.4g total fat (28.2g saturated fat); 3298kJ (789 cal); 53.5g carbohydrate; 11.8g protein; 4.3g fibre

sweet almond cherry tarts

1½ cups (225g) plain flour
150g butter, chopped coarsely
⅓ cup (55g) icing sugar
2 tablespoons iced water, approximately
2⅓ cups (350g) cherries, seeded
2 tablespoons white sugar
almond filling
60g butter, softened
⅓ cup (75g) firmly packed brown sugar
1 egg
1 tablespoon plain flour
1 cup (100g) ground almonds

1 Process flour, butter and icing sugar until mixture resembles breadcrumbs. Add enough of the water, if needed, processing until mixture just comes together. Knead on floured surface until smooth. Enclose in plastic wrap; refrigerate 30 minutes.
2 Preheat oven to 200°C/180°C fan-forced. Grease four oven trays; line with baking paper.
3 Make almond filling.
4 Divide pastry into eight pieces. Roll each piece into 15cm-round on floured surface; place two rounds on each tray. Divide almond filling among rounds, leaving a 4cm border. Top with cherries; fold over border. Sprinkle with white sugar.
5 Bake tarts about 20 minutes or until pastry is browned lightly. Serve with thick cream or vanilla ice-cream, if you like.
almond filling Beat butter, sugar and egg in small bowl with electric mixer until smooth. Stir in flour and ground almonds.

prep + cook time 45 minutes (+ refrigeration) **makes** 8
nutritional count per tart 29.5g total fat (14.9g saturated fat); 1990kJ (476 cal); 44.6g carbohydrate; 7g protein; 2.7g fibre

chocolate jaffa tart

1½ cups (225g) plain flour
¼ cup (40g) icing sugar
125g cold unsalted butter, chopped
2 egg yolks
2 teaspoons iced water, approximately
3 eggs
1 tablespoon finely grated orange rind
⅔ cup (160ml) thickened cream

¾ cup (165g) caster sugar
60g dark eating chocolate, melted
2 tablespoons cocoa powder
2 tablespoons grand marnier
140g dark eating chocolate, chopped coarsely, extra
¼ cup (60ml) thickened cream, extra
20 Ferrero Rocher chocolates, halved

1 Grease 24cm-round loose-based flan tin.
2 Blend or process flour, icing sugar and butter until crumbly. Add egg yolks and enough of the water to make ingredients just come together. Knead pastry on floured surface until smooth. Enclose with plastic wrap; refrigerate 30 minutes.
3 Roll pastry, between sheets of baking paper, until large enough to line tin. Lift pastry into tin, press into base and side; trim edge. Cover; refrigerate 30 minutes.
4 Preheat oven to 200°C/180°C fan-forced.
5 Place tin on oven tray; line pastry with baking paper, fill with dried beans or rice. Bake 10 minutes; remove paper and beans. Bake further 10 minutes or until pastry is browned lightly; cool. Reduce oven to 180°C/160°C fan-forced.
6 Meanwhile, whisk whole eggs, rind, cream, caster sugar, chocolate, sifted cocoa powder and liqueur in medium bowl until combined. Pour chocolate mixture into pastry case.
7 Bake tart about 30 minutes or until filling is set; cool.
8 Stir extra chocolate and extra cream in small saucepan over low heat until smooth. Spread warm chocolate mixture over top of cold tart; refrigerate until set. Decorate with Ferrero Rocher halves.

prep + cook time 1 hour 20 minutes (+ refrigeration) **serves** 8
nutritional count per serving 46.7g total fat (23.1g saturated fat); 3269kJ (782 cal); 77.6g carbohydrate; 12.1g protein; 2.7g fibre

portuguese custard tarts

½ cup (110g) caster sugar
2 tablespoons cornflour
3 egg yolks
¾ cup (180ml) milk
½ cup (125ml) cream
1 vanilla bean, split lengthways
5cm strip lemon rind
1 sheet butter puff pastry

1 Preheat oven to 220°C/200°C fan-forced. Grease two 12-hole
(1 tablespoon/20ml) mini muffin pans.
2 Combine sugar and cornflour in medium saucepan. Gradually whisk
in combined egg yolks, milk and cream.
3 Scrape vanilla bean seeds into custard; add rind. Stir over medium
heat until mixture just comes to the boil. Remove from heat; discard rind.
Cover surface of custard with plastic wrap while making pastry cases.
4 Cut pastry sheet in half; place two halves on top of each other. Roll
pastry up tightly from long side; cut log into 24 rounds. Roll each round
on floured surface to 6cm diameter; press into pan holes.
5 Spoon custard into pastry cases. Bake about 12 minutes. Turn, top-side
up, onto wire rack to cool. Serve dusted with a little sifted icing sugar.

prep + cook time 45 minutes (+ standing) **makes** 24
nutritional count per tart 4.8g total fat (2.7g saturated fat);
339kJ (81 cal); 8.3g carbohydrate; 1.1g protein; 0.1g fibre

caramel tartlets

18 (220g) butternut snap biscuits
395g can sweetened condensed milk
60g butter, chopped coarsely
⅓ cup (75g) firmly packed brown sugar
1 tablespoon lemon juice

1 Preheat oven to 160°C/140°C fan-forced. Grease two 12-hole
(1½ tablespoons/30ml) shallow round-based patty pans.
2 Place one biscuit each over top of 18 pan holes. Bake about 4 minutes
or until biscuits soften. Using the back of a teaspoon, gently press
softened biscuits into pan holes; cool.
3 Stir condensed milk, butter and sugar in small heavy-based saucepan
over heat until smooth. Bring to the boil; boil, stirring, about 10 minutes
or until mixture is thick and dark caramel in colour. Remove from heat;
stir in juice.
4 Spoon caramel mixture into biscuit cases; refrigerate 30 minutes or
until set.

prep + cook time 35 minutes (+ standing) **makes** 18
nutritional count per tartlet 7.7g total fat (5g saturated fat);
727kJ (174 cal); 23.2g carbohydrate; 2.6g protein; 0.4g fibre

chocolate tartlets

150g dark eating chocolate
¼ cup (60ml) thickened cream
1 tablespoon orange-flavoured liqueur
1 egg
2 egg yolks
2 tablespoons caster sugar
pastry
1⅔ cups (250g) plain flour
⅓ cup (75g) caster sugar
150g cold butter, chopped coarsely
1 egg yolk
2 teaspoons water

1 Make pastry.
2 Grease two 12-hole (2 tablespoons/40ml) deep flat-based patty pans.
3 Roll pastry between sheets of baking paper to 3mm thickness;
cut out 24 x 6.5cm rounds. Press rounds into pan holes; prick bases
all over with fork. Refrigerate 30 minutes.
4 Preheat oven to 200°C/180°C fan-forced.
5 Bake pastry cases 10 minutes. Cool.
6 Reduce oven to 180°C/160°C fan-forced.
7 Stir chocolate, cream and liqueur in small saucepan over low heat
until smooth. Cool 5 minutes.
8 Meanwhile, beat egg, egg yolks and sugar in small bowl with electric
mixer until light and fluffy; fold chocolate mixture into egg mixture.
Spoon filling into pastry cases.
9 Bake tartlets 8 minutes; cool 10 minutes. Refrigerate 1 hour.
Serve dusted with a little sifted cocoa powder.
pastry Process flour, sugar and butter until coarse. Add egg yolk and
the water; process until combined. Knead pastry on floured surface until
smooth. Enclose in plastic wrap; refrigerate 30 minutes.

prep + cook time 35 minutes (+ refrigeration) **makes** 24
nutritional count per tartlet 8.9g total fat (5.4g saturated fat);
656kJ (157 cal); 16.5g carbohydrate; 2.2g protein; 0.5g fibre

blood orange meringue pies

½ cup (110g) caster sugar
2 tablespoons cornflour
⅔ cup (160ml) blood orange juice
2 tablespoons water
2 teaspoons finely grated
    blood orange rind
75g unsalted butter,
    chopped coarsely
2 eggs, separated
½ cup (110g) caster sugar, extra

pastry
1¼ cups (185g) plain flour
¼ cup (55g) caster sugar
125g cold butter, chopped coarsely
1 egg yolk
2 teaspoons water

1 Make pastry.
2 Grease 12-hole (⅓-cup/80ml) muffin pan. Roll pastry between sheets of baking paper to 4mm thickness; cut out 12 x 8cm rounds. Press rounds into pan holes; prick bases all over with fork. Refrigerate 30 minutes.
3 Preheat oven to 200°C/180°C fan-forced.
4 Bake pastry cases 10 minutes. Cool.
5 Meanwhile, combine sugar and cornflour in small saucepan; gradually stir in juice and the water until smooth. Cook, stirring, until mixture boils and thickens. Reduce heat; simmer, stirring, 1 minute. Remove from heat; stir in rind, butter and egg yolks. Cool 10 minutes.
6 Spoon filling into pastry cases. Refrigerate 1 hour.
7 Increase oven to 240°C/220°C fan-forced.
8 Beat egg whites in small bowl with electric mixer until soft peaks form; gradually add extra sugar, beating until sugar dissolves.
9 Roughen surface of filling with fork; using star nozzle, pipe meringue over filling. Bake about 3 minutes or until browned lightly.
pastry Process flour, sugar and butter until coarse. Add egg yolk and the water; process until combined. Knead on floured surface until smooth. Enclose in plastic wrap; refrigerate 30 minutes.

prep + cook time 45 minutes (+ refrigeration) **makes** 12
nutritional count per pie 15.3g total fat (9.5g saturated fat); 1250kJ (299 cal); 36.7 carbohydrate; 3.2g protein; 0.6g fibre

baklava figs

6 sheets fillo pastry
50g butter, melted
12 large fresh figs (960g)
⅓ cup (75g) firmly packed brown sugar
1 teaspoon mixed spice
½ teaspoon ground cinnamon
80g butter, chopped coarsely
½ cup (60g) finely chopped roasted walnuts
¼ cup (35g) slivered almonds
1 teaspoon finely grated orange rind
maple cream
300ml thickened cream
2 tablespoons maple syrup

1 Preheat oven to 200°C/180°C fan-forced. Grease 12-hole (⅓-cup/ 80ml) muffin pan.
2 Brush three pastry sheets with melted butter; stack together. Repeat with remaining pastry. Cut each pastry stack into six rectangles (you will have 12 rectangles). Gently press one stack into each pan hole.
3 Quarter each fig, cutting three-quarters of the way down the fig. Place one fig in each pastry case.
4 Combine sugar and spices in medium bowl; rub in chopped butter. Stir in nuts and rind; gently push mixture into the centre of figs.
5 Bake baklava figs about 15 minutes.
6 Meanwhile, make maple cream.
7 Serve baklava figs, dusted with a little sifted icing sugar, and maple cream.
maple cream Beat cream and syrup in small bowl with electric mixer until soft peaks form.

prep + cook time 45 minutes **makes** 12
nutritional count per baklava 23.7g total fat (12.3g saturated fat); 1308kJ (313 cal); 20.5g carbohydrate; 3.7g protein; 2.7g fibre

caramel cashew tarts

1 cup (150g) roasted unsalted cashews
1 tablespoon cornflour
¾ cup (165g) firmly packed rown sugar
2 tablespoons golden syrup
50g butter, melted
2 eggs
2 tablespoons cream
1 teaspoon vanilla extract

pastry
1¼ cups (185g) plain flour
¼ cup (55g) caster sugar
125g cold butter, chopped coarsely
1 egg yolk
2 teaspoons water
cinnamon cream
300ml thickened cream
1 tablespoon icing sugar
1 teaspoon ground cinnamon

1 Make pastry.
2 Grease two 12-hole (⅓-cup/80ml) muffin pans. Roll pastry between sheets of baking paper to 3mm thickness; cut out 24 x 8cm rounds. Press rounds into pan holes; prick bases all over with fork. Refrigerate 20 minutes.
3 Preheat oven to 200°C/180°C fan-forced.
4 Bake pastry cases 10 minutes. Cool.
5 Reduce oven to 160°C/140°C fan-forced.
6 Combine nuts and cornflour in medium bowl; stir in sugar, syrup, butter, egg, cream and extract. Spoon filling into pastry cases.
7 Bake tarts about 15 minutes; cool. Refrigerate 30 minutes.
8 Meanwhile, make cinnamon cream.
9 Serve tarts with cinnamon cream.
pastry Process flour, sugar and butter until coarse. Add egg yolk and the water; process until combined. Knead on floured surface until smooth. Enclose in plastic wrap; refrigerate 30 minutes.
cinnamon cream Beat ingredients in small bowl with electric mixer until soft peaks form.

prep + cook time 45 minutes (+ refrigeration) **makes** 24
nutritional count per tart 15.2g total fat (8.2g saturated fat); 932kJ (223 cal); 18.6g carbohydrate; 29g protein; 0.7g fibre

crème brûlée praline tarts

1⅓ cups (330ml) cream
⅓ cup (80ml) milk
1 vanilla bean
4 egg yolks
¼ cup (55g) caster sugar
pastry
1¼ cups (185g) plain flour
¼ cup (55g) caster sugar
125g cold butter, chopped coarsely
1 egg yolk
2 teaspoons water

praline
¼ cup (55g) caster sugar
2 tablespoons water
1 tablespoon roasted hazelnuts
2 tablespoons roasted
  unsalted pistachios

1 Make pastry.
2 Grease six-hole (¾-cup/180ml) texas muffin pan. Cut six 11cm rounds from pastry. Press rounds into pan holes; prick bases all over with fork. Refrigerate 30 minutes.
3 Preheat oven to 160°C/140°C fan-forced.
4 Combine cream and milk in small saucepan. Split vanilla bean in half lengthways; scrape seeds into pan (reserve pod for another use). Bring to the boil. Beat egg yolks and sugar in small bowl with electric mixer until thick and creamy. Gradually whisk hot cream mixture into egg mixture. Pour warm custard into pastry cases.
5 Bake tarts 30 minutes or until set; cool 15 minutes. Refrigerate 1 hour.
6 Meanwhile, make praline.
7 Preheat grill. Remove tarts from pan; place on oven tray. Sprinkle custard with praline; grill until praline caramelises. Serve immediately.
pastry Process flour, sugar and butter until coarse. Add yolk and the water; process until combined. Knead on floured surface until smooth. Roll pastry between sheets of baking paper to 4mm thickness. Refrigerate 15 minutes.
praline Stir sugar and the water in small saucepan over heat until sugar dissolves. Boil, uncovered, without stirring, 8 minutes or until golden. Place nuts, in single layer, on greased oven tray. Pour toffee over nuts; stand 15 minutes or until set. Break toffee into large pieces; process until chopped finely.

prep + cook time 1 hour (+ refrigeration & standing) **makes** 6
nutritional count per tart 49.8g total fat (29.1g saturated fat); 2901kJ (694 cal); 52.8g carbohydrate; 8.7g protein; 1.8g fibre

baby tartlets with fruit

1½ cups (225g) plain flour
2 tablespoons icing sugar
125g cold butter, chopped
1 egg yolk
3 teaspoons iced water, approximately
1 cup (250ml) crème fraîche
2 tablespoons icing sugar, extra

1 Sift flour and icing sugar into bowl, rub in butter. Add egg yolk and enough water to make ingredients cling together. Press dough into a ball, knead gently on floured surface until smooth. Wrap in plastic; refrigerate 30 minutes.
2 Preheat oven to 180°C/160°C fan-forced.
3 Divide pastry in half. Roll each half between sheets of baking paper until 3mm thick; cut out 48 x 4.5cm rounds. Place rounds into four 12-hole (2 teaspoon/10ml) tiny tartlet tins. Prick pastry with fork.
4 Bake pastry cases 15 minutes or until lightly browned; cool.
5 Top pastry cases with 1 teaspoon of combined crème fraîche and icing sugar. Decorate with fruit, as desired; dust with a little sifted icing sugar.

prep + cook time 45 minutes (+ refrigeration) **makes** 48
nutritional count per tartlet 4.4g total fat (2.8g saturated fat); 238kJ (57 cal); 3.8g carbohydrate; 0.7g protein; 0.2g fibre
tip Pastry cases can be made 3 days ahead; store in airtight container.

neenish tarts

1½ cups (225g) plain flour
100g cold butter, chopped
1 egg yolk
1 tablespoon lemon juice
1 tablespoon iced water,
  approximately

mock cream
½ cup (110g) caster sugar
⅓ cup (80ml) water
125g soft butter
1 teaspoon vanilla extract

glacé icing
1½ cups (240g) icing sugar
2 tablespoons milk
½ teaspoon vanilla extract
1½ tablespoons cocoa
1½ teaspoons milk, extra

1 Grease two 12-hole tartlet trays (patty pans).
2 Sift flour into bowl; rub in butter. Add egg yolk, juice and enough water to make ingredients cling together. Press dough into a ball, knead gently on floured surface until smooth. Wrap in plastic; refrigerate 30 minutes.
3 Roll pastry on floured surface until 2mm thick, cut into 7cm rounds. Line trays with pastry rounds; prick pastry all over with fork. Refrigerate 30 minutes.
4 Meanwhile, make mock cream. Make glacé icing.
5 Preheat oven to 180°C/160°C fan-forced. Bake pastry cases about 12 minutes or until lightly browned. Lift cases onto wire racks to cool.
6 Fill pastry cases with mock cream, level with spatula. Spread a teaspoon of vanilla icing over half of each tart; allow to set. Cover remaining half of each tart with chocolate icing.
mock cream Stir sugar and the water in small saucepan over heat, without boiling, until sugar dissolves. Bring to the boil; remove from heat, cool. Beat butter and extract in small bowl with electric mixer until as white as possible, gradually beat in cooled syrup; beat until light and fluffy.
glacé icing Sift sugar into small bowl, stir in milk and extract; beat until smooth. Divide mixture into two small heatproof bowls. Stir sifted cocoa and extra milk into one bowl. Stir each bowl of icing over small saucepan of simmering water until smooth and spreadable.

prep + cook time 1 hour 20 minutes (+ refrigeration) **makes** 24
nutritional count per tart 8.1g total fat (5.2g saturated fat);
677kJ (162 cal); 21.6g carbohydrate; 1.3g protein; 0.4g fibre
tip Add ½ teaspoon jam to each case before filling with mock cream.

gluten-free lemon tarts

1¼ cups (225g) rice flour
¼ cup (35g) (corn) cornflour
¼ cup (30g) soya flour
⅓ cup (75g) caster sugar
150g cold butter, chopped coarsely
¼ cup (60ml) cold water,
approximately
1 tablespoon pure icing sugar

lemon filling
1 cup (250g) mascarpone cheese
4 eggs
½ cup (80g) pure icing sugar
1 tablespoon finely grated
lemon rind
½ cup (125ml) lemon juice

1 Process flours, caster sugar and butter until crumbly; add enough of the water to make ingredients come together. Knead dough gently on floured surface until smooth.

2 Preheat oven to 180°C/160°C fan-forced. Grease six 10cm deep loose-based flan tins.

3 Divide pastry into six portions. Roll one portion at a time between sheets of baking paper until large enough to line tins. Ease pastry into tins, pressing into base and side; trim edges, prick base with fork. Cover; refrigerate 30 minutes.

4 Place tins on oven tray; line pastry with baking paper, fill with dried beans or rice. Bake 10 minutes; remove paper and beans. Bake further 10 minutes; cool.

5 Reduce oven to 160°C/140°C fan-forced.

6 Make lemon filling; spoon filling into pastry cases.

7 Bake tarts about 30 minutes or until the surface is firm to touch. Remove from oven; cool. Refrigerate 2 hours before serving dusted with sifted icing sugar.

lemon filling Whisk mascarpone and eggs together in large jug until smooth. Add sifted sugar, rind and juice; whisk until smooth.

prep + cook time 1 hour 15 minutes (+ standing & refrigeration)
makes 6
nutritional count per tart 45.4g total fat (28.4g saturated fat); 3043kJ (728 cal); 68.6g carbohydrate; 11g protein; 1.5g fibre
tip This recipe is also wheat-free, yeast-free and nut-free.

spiced apple and fruit mince tarts

1 sheet shortcrust pastry
½ cup (150g) fruit mince
1 medium apple (150g), peeled, cored, sliced thinly
1 egg
2 teaspoons white sugar
½ teaspoon mixed spice

1 Preheat oven to 200°C/180°C fan-forced. Line oven tray with baking paper.
2 Cut pastry sheet into quarters. Fold 1cm border around each pastry square; press firmly. Place pastry squares on oven tray.
3 Spread fruit mince in centre of each square; top with apple. Brush apples with egg; sprinkle with combined sugar and spice.
4 Bake tarts about 20 minutes. Serve with custard, if you like.

prep + cook time 35 minutes **serves** 4
nutritional count per serve 14g total fat (6.8g saturated fat); 1346kJ (322 cal); 42.7g carbohydrate; 4.9g protein; 2.5g fibre

lemon meringue tarts

12 (275g) small frozen sweet tart cases
340g jar lemon curd
3 egg whites
¾ cup (165g) caster sugar

1 Preheat oven to 180°C/160°C fan-forced.
2 Place tart cases on oven tray; bake cases 10 minutes, cool. Increase oven to 240°C/220°C fan-forced.
3 Spoon lemon curd into tart cases.
4 Beat egg whites in small bowl with electric mixer until soft peaks form; gradually add sugar, beating until dissolved between additions. Pipe or spoon meringue over lemon curd.
5 Bake tarts about 5 minutes or until meringue is browned lightly.

prep + cook time 15 minutes **makes** 12
nutritional count per tart 14g total fat (6.2g saturated fat); 1254kJ (300 cal); 40.3g carbohydrate; 4g protein; 0.6g fibre

gluten-free custard tarts

1½ cups (120g) desiccated coconut
1½ cups (115g) shredded coconut
⅔ cup (150g) caster sugar
4 egg whites, beaten lightly
3 egg yolks
½ cup (110g) caster sugar, extra
1 tablespoon arrowroot
¾ cup (180ml) milk
½ cup (125ml) cream
1 vanilla bean
5cm strip lemon rind
1 tablespoon pure icing sugar

1 Preheat oven to 180°C/160°C fan-forced. Grease 12-hole (⅓-cup/80ml) muffin pan.
2 Combine coconuts and sugar in large bowl; stir in egg whites. Press mixture over base and side of pan holes to make cases.
3 Whisk egg yolks, extra sugar and arrowroot together in medium saucepan; gradually whisk in milk and cream to make custard.
4 Split vanilla bean in half lengthways; scrape seeds into custard, discard pod. Add lemon rind to custard; stir over medium heat until mixture boils and thickens slightly. Remove from heat immediately; discard rind.
5 Spoon warm custard into pastry cases; bake about 15 minutes or until set and browned lightly. Stand tarts in pan 10 minutes. Transfer to wire rack to cool.
6 Serve tarts dusted with sifted icing sugar.

prep + cook time 45 minutes (+ standing & cooling) **makes** 12
nutritional count per tart 19.3g total fat (15.1g saturated fat);
1233kJ (295 cal); 25.4g carbohydrate; 3.9g protein; 2.9g fibre
tip This recipe is also wheat-free and yeast-free.

fruit mince tarts

2 cups (300g) plain flour
2 tablespoons custard powder
⅓ cup (75g) caster sugar
185g cold butter, chopped
1 egg yolk
2 tablespoons cold water,
  approximately
1 egg white, beaten lightly
1 tablespoon sugar

fruit mince filling
475g jar fruit mince
2 tablespoons brandy
¼ cup (35g) glacé peaches,
  chopped
¼ cup (35g) glacé apricots,
  chopped
1 teaspoon grated orange rind
2 teaspoons grated lemon rind

1 Grease two 12-hole deep patty pan trays.
2 Blend or process flour, custard powder, sugar and butter until combined. Add egg yolk and enough of the water to make ingredients just come together. Knead dough on floured surface until smooth. Enclose in plastic wrap; refrigerate 30 minutes.
3 Roll two-thirds of the dough between sheets of baking paper until 3mm thick. Cut 24 x 7.5cm rounds from pastry, re-roll pastry if necessary to make 24 rounds. Place rounds into trays; reserve pastry scraps. Cover; refrigerate until required.
4 Make fruit mince filling.
5 Preheat oven to 200°C/180°C fan-forced.
6 Spoon 1 heaped teaspoon of fruit mince filling into pastry cases. Roll remaining pastry until 3mm thick. Using 4.5cm star and Christmas tree cutters, cut out 12 stars and 12 trees. Place pastry shapes in centre of tarts; brush with egg white, sprinkle with sugar.
7 Bake tarts about 20 minutes or until browned lightly.
fruit mince filling Combine ingredients in medium bowl.

prep + cook time 1 hour (+ refrigeration) **makes** 24
nutritional count per tart 7.3g total fat (4.4g saturated fat); 748kJ (179 cal); 25.8g carbohydrate; 1.9g protein; 1.1g fibre

lime meringue tartlets

2 eggs, separated
2 tablespoons caster sugar
1 teaspoon finely grated lime rind
1½ tablespoons lime juice
20g butter
½ cup (110g) caster sugar, extra
⅔ cup (50g) shredded coconut
20 x 4cm shortcrust pastry cases

1 Combine egg yolks, sugar, rind, juice and butter in small heatproof bowl. Stir constantly over small saucepan of simmering water until mixture thickens slightly and coats the back of a spoon; remove from heat. Cover; refrigerate curd until cold.
2 Preheat oven to 220°C/200°C fan-forced.
3 Beat egg whites in small bowl with electric mixer until soft peaks form; gradually add extra sugar, 1 tablespoon at a time, beating until sugar dissolves between additions. Gently fold in ½ cup (35g) of the coconut.
4 Spoon curd into pastry cases; spoon meringue evenly over curd to enclose filling. Sprinkle tarts with remaining coconut.
5 Bake tartlets about 5 minutes or until meringue is browned lightly. Refrigerate until ready to serve.

prep + cook time 45 minutes (+ refrigeration) **makes** 20
nutritional count per tartlet 5.3g total fat (3.4g saturated fat); 405kJ (97 cal); 11.1g carbohydrate; 1.5g protein; 0.5g fibre

lemon delicious tartlets

1 sheet butter puff pastry
20g butter, melted
1 teaspoon caster sugar
2 tablespoons icing sugar
1 egg, separated
⅓ cup (75g) caster sugar, extra

10g butter, melted, extra
⅓ cup (80ml) milk
1 teaspoon finely grated lemon rind
1½ tablespoons lemon juice
2 tablespoons self-raising flour

1 Cut pastry sheet in half; stand on board 5 minutes or until partially thawed. Grease a 12-hole, deep patty pan tray with a pastry brush dipped in the melted butter. Cut 12 x 10cm squares of baking paper.
2 Sprinkle one half of pastry with caster sugar, top with remaining pastry half. Roll pastry stack up tightly from short side. Refrigerate until firm.
3 Cut pastry log into 12 x 1cm-wide pieces. Place one pastry piece, spiral-side down, on an icing sugar dusted board; refrigerate remaining pastry pieces. Roll out pastry piece to about 10cm round. Cut out a round from pastry using a 9cm cutter. Press round into a pan hole. Repeat with remaining pastry pieces. Freeze 10 minutes.
4 Preheat oven to 220°C/200°C fan-forced.
5 Line pastry in pan with baking paper squares; place about a tablespoon of dried beans or rice. Bake 10 minutes; remove paper and beans. Reduce oven to 160°C/140°C fan-forced; bake further 10 minutes or until base of pastry is browned lightly and crisp. Cool. Reduce oven to 150°C/130°C fan-forced.
6 Meanwhile, beat egg yolk and 2 tablespoons of the extra sugar in a small bowl with an electric mixer until thick and creamy; fold in extra butter, milk, rind and juice, then sifted flour.
7 Beat egg white in small bowl with electric mixer until soft peaks form; gradually beat in remaining extra sugar until sugar dissolves. Fold into lemon mixture, in two batches. Spoon mixture into pastry cases.
8 Bake tartlets 10 minutes or until just set. Remove tartlets from pan; cool on a wire rack. Serve dusted with sifted icing sugar, if you like.

prep + cook time 1 hour (+ refrigeration) **makes** 12
nutritional count per tartlet 6g total fat (3.4g saturated fat); 506kJ (121 cal); 15.2g carbohydrate; 1.9g protein; 0.3g fibre

divine chocolate and raspberry tarts

125g unsalted butter
½ cup (50g) cocoa powder
⅓ cup (110g) raspberry jam
⅔ cup (150g) caster sugar
2 eggs, beaten lightly
⅔ cup (100g) plain flour
pinch bicarbonate of soda
125g cream cheese, softened
1 egg yolk
½ cup (75g) frozen raspberries

1 Preheat oven to 160°C/140°C fan-forced. Grease six 10cm-round, loose-based flan tins; place on oven tray.
2 Melt butter in medium saucepan. Whisk in sifted cocoa over low heat until mixture boils. Remove from heat; whisk in jam and ½ cup of the sugar. Stir in eggs, then sifted flour and soda. Divide mixture among tins.
3 Beat cheese, remaining sugar and egg yolk in small bowl with electric mixer until smooth; stir in raspberries.
4 Drop spoonfuls of cheese mixture over the chocolate mixture; pull a knife backwards and forwards several times through mixture for a marbled effect.
5 Bake tarts about 30 minutes. Serve warm or cold with whipped cream, if you like.

prep + cook time 1 hour **makes** 6
nutritional count per tart 28.4g total fat (17.4g saturated fat);
2073kJ (496 cal); 52.7g carbohydrate; 8.5g protein; 2g fibre

pear, rhubarb and ricotta tarts

1¼ cups (250g) low-fat ricotta cheese
2 egg yolks
2 tablespoons caster sugar
2 teaspoons plain flour
½ cup (55g) finely chopped rhubarb
1 small pear (180g), quartered, sliced thinly lengthways
1 tablespoon caster sugar, extra

1 Preheat oven to 200°C/180°C fan-forced. Grease four 10cm-round deep fluted tins; place on oven tray.
2 Beat cheese, egg yolks, sugar and flour in small bowl with electric mixer until smooth; stir in rhubarb. Spread mixture into tins; top each with pear, sprinkle with extra sugar.
3 Bake tarts about 25 minutes. Cool 10 minutes. Refrigerate until cold.

prep + cook time 40 minutes (+ refrigeration) **makes** 4
nutritional count per tart 7.9g total fat (4.2g saturated fat);
769kJ (184 cal); 20.3g carbohydrate; 8.3g protein; 1.3g fibre

pear, chocolate and almond galette

80g dark eating chocolate, chopped finely
¼ cup (30g) ground almonds
1 sheet puff pastry, thawed
1 tablespoon milk
1 medium pear (230g)
1 tablespoon raw sugar

1 Preheat oven to 220°C/200°C fan-forced. Grease oven tray; line with baking paper.
2 Combine chocolate and 2 tablespoons of the ground almonds in small bowl.
3 Cut pastry sheet into quarters; place quarters on oven tray, prick each with a fork, brush with milk. Divide chocolate mixture over pastry squares, leaving 2cm border.
4 Peel and core pear; cut into quarters. Cut each pear quarter into thin slices then spread one sliced pear quarter across each pastry square; sprinkle with sugar then remaining ground nuts. Bake about 15 minutes.

prep + cook time 20 minutes **serves** 4
nutritional count per serving 19.6g total fat (4.5g saturated fat); 1455kJ (348 cal); 38g carbohydrate; 5.2g protein; 2.2g fibre

caramelised apple tarts

50g butter
¼ cup (55g) firmly packed brown sugar
½ teaspoon ground cinnamon
4 small apples (520g), peeled, cored, sliced thinly
½ cup (50g) roasted pecans
¼ cup (75g) apple sauce
2 teaspoons lemon juice
2 sheets butter puff pastry, thawed
1 egg

1 Stir butter, sugar and cinnamon in large frying pan over low heat until sugar dissolves. Add apple; cook, stirring occasionally, over low heat, until apple softens. Drain apple mixture over medium bowl; reserve caramel syrup.
2 Meanwhile, blend or process nuts, apple sauce and juice until smooth.
3 Preheat oven to 200°C/180°C fan-forced. Grease oven tray; line with baking paper.
4 Cut eight 11cm rounds from pastry sheets. Place four of the rounds on oven tray; brush with egg. Using 9cm cutter, remove centres from four remaining rounds; centre pastry rings on 11cm rounds. Spread nut mixture in centre of rounds; top with apple.
5 Bake tarts about 15 minutes. Serve tarts warm with warmed reserved caramel syrup.

prep + cook time 30 minutes **makes** 4
nutritional count per tart 39.8g total fat (18g saturated fat); 2642kJ (632 cal); 60.5g carbohydrate; 8.3g protein; 4.3g fibre
tip Apple sauce can be bought from supermarkets. However, you can stew and puree your own apples if you like, or, buy canned apple usually sold for babies. Any of the above will be fine for this recipe.

chocolate butterscotch tartlets

12 frozen tartlet cases
¼ cup (55g) firmly packed brown sugar
20g butter
¼ cup (60ml) cream
150g dark eating chocolate, chopped coarsely
¼ cup (60ml) cream, extra
2 tablespoons coarsely chopped roasted hazelnuts
1 tablespoon cocoa powder

1 Bake tartlet cases according to manufacturer's instructions.
2 Meanwhile, stir sugar, butter and cream in small saucepan until sugar dissolves. Reduce heat; simmer, uncovered, without stirring, 2 minutes. Cool 5 minutes. Stir in chocolate and extra cream; refrigerate 10 minutes.
3 Spoon mixture into tartlet cases; sprinkle with nuts and sifted cocoa.

prep + cook time 15 minutes (+ refrigeration) **makes** 12
nutritional count per tartlet 16.1g total fat (9g saturated fat); 1003kJ (240 cal); 22g carbohydrate; 2.6g protein; 0.7g fibre

passionfruit curd tartlets

4 egg yolks
½ cup (110g) caster sugar
80g butter, softened
1 cup (250ml) passionfruit pulp
1 teaspoon gelatine
2 tablespoons water
½ cup (125ml) thickened cream

pastry
1⅔ cups (250g) plain flour
½ cup (110g) caster sugar
140g cold butter, chopped coarsely
1 egg, beaten lightly
2 teaspoons iced water
berry topping
¼ cup (80g) raspberry jam
1 tablespoon water
150g blueberries

1 Make pastry.
2 Divide pastry into eight portions; roll portions between sheets of baking paper, into rounds large enough to line eight 10cm-round loose-based flan tins. Lift rounds into tins; press into sides, trim edges, prick bases all over with fork. Refrigerate 20 minutes.
3 Preheat oven to 180°C/160°C fan-forced. Place tins on oven tray. Line each with baking paper; fill with dried beans or rice. Bake 15 minutes. Remove paper and beans; bake further 7 minutes. Cool.
4 Meanwhile, stir yolks, sugar, butter and ⅓ cup of the pulp in medium heatproof bowl over medium saucepan of simmering water; cook, stirring, 10 minutes or until curd coats the back of a spoon. Strain; discard seeds.
5 Sprinkle gelatine over the water in small heatproof jug. Stand jug in small saucepan of simmering water; stir until gelatine dissolves. Stir gelatine mixture and remaining pulp into warm curd. Cover; refrigerate 1 hour.
6 Meanwhile, make berry topping.
7 Beat cream in small bowl with electric mixer until soft peaks form; fold into curd mixture. Divide curd filling among pastry cases; refrigerate until firm. Serve tartlets with berry topping.
pastry Process flour, sugar and butter until crumbly. Add egg and enough of the water until ingredients come together. Knead pastry on floured surface until smooth. Enclose in plastic wrap; refrigerate 30 minutes.
berry topping Combine jam and the water in small saucepan over medium heat; simmer, stirring, until reduced by half. Push mixture through sieve into small bowl, gently stir in berries.

prep + cook time 1 hour (+ refrigeration) **makes** 8
nutritional count per tartlet 32.9g total fat (20.3g saturated fat); 2404kJ (575 cal); 61.2g carbohydrate; 7.5g protein; 6g fibre

sticky pecan tarts

3 sheets puff pastry
cooking-oil spray
60g butter
2 tablespoons brown sugar
2 tablespoons light corn syrup
1 tablespoon maple syrup
1 cup (120g) roasted pecans
⅓ cup (25g) shredded coconut, toasted
1 teaspoon ground nutmeg

1 Preheat oven to 220°C/200°C fan-forced. Grease 12-hole (⅓-cup/ 80ml) muffin pan.
2 Cut 12 x 8cm rounds from pastry. Place rounds in pan holes; prick bases with fork, spray with cooking-oil spray. Top with another muffin pan; bake 5 minutes. Remove top pan; bake further 2 minutes.
3 Meanwhile, combine butter, sugar and syrups in medium saucepan; cook, stirring, without boiling, until sugar dissolves. Bring to the simmer; cook 5 minutes. Stir in nuts, coconut and nutmeg.
4 Spoon nut mixture into pastry cases; bake tarts about 5 minutes.

prep + cook time 25 minutes **makes** 12
nutritional count per tart 22.5g total fat (9.5g saturated fat); 1287kJ (308 cal); 22.8g carbohydrate; 3.5g protein; 1.7g fibre

banana and passionfruit flans

1¼ cups (185g) plain flour
2 tablespoons icing sugar
125g butter, chopped
1 egg yolk
1 teaspoon water, approximately
5 medium bananas (1kg)
⅓ cup (80ml) passionfruit pulp

creamy custard filling
8 egg yolks
1 cup (220g) caster sugar
2 tablespoons cornflour
2 cups (500ml) milk
2 teaspoons vanilla extract

1 Sift flour and icing sugar into bowl; rub in butter. Stir in egg yolk and enough water to make ingredients cling together. Knead gently on floured surface until smooth. Cover, refrigerate 30 minutes.
2 Meanwhile, make creamy custard filling.
3 Preheat oven to 200°C/180°C fan-forced.
4 Divide pastry into six equal portions. Roll each portion between sheets of baking paper until large enough to line one of six 10cm loose-based flan tins. Ease pastry into tins, press base and side; trim edges. Prick pastry all over with a fork; bake about 15 minutes or until golden brown. Cool 5 minutes, remove cases from tins.
5 Peel and thinly slice bananas on the diagonal.
6 Divide custard among pastry cases. Arrange banana slices on top of flans. Brush passionfruit pulp over banana slices. Refrigerate until ready to serve.
creamy custard filling Whisk egg yolks, sugar and cornflour together in bowl until thick. Heat milk in small saucepan, gradually stir in egg yolk mixture, stirring constantly, over heat until mixture boils and thickens. Stir in extract; cover to prevent skin forming, cool. Refrigerate until cold.

prep + cook time 50 minutes (+ refrigeration) **makes** 6
nutritional count per flan 29.3g total fat (16g saturated fat); 2926kJ (700 cal); 92.7g carbohydrate; 13.3g protein; 5.5g fibre

pecan, macadamia and walnut tartlets

1¼ cups (185g) plain flour
⅓ cup (55g) icing sugar
¼ cup (30g) ground almonds
125g cold butter, chopped
1 egg yolk

filling
⅓ cup (50g) roasted macadamias
⅓ cup (35g) roasted pecans
⅓ cup (35g) roasted walnuts
2 tablespoons brown sugar
1 tablespoon plain flour
40g butter, melted
2 eggs, beaten lightly
¾ cup (180ml) maple syrup

1 Grease four 10cm-round loose-based flan tins.
2 Blend or process flour, sugar and ground nuts with butter until combined. Add egg yolk; process until ingredients just come together. Knead pastry on floured surface until smooth. Enclose with plastic wrap; refrigerate 30 minutes.
3 Divide pastry into quarters. Roll each piece, between sheets of baking paper, into rounds large enough to line tins. Lift pastry into each tin, press into sides; trim edges. Cover; refrigerate 1 hour.
4 Preheat oven to 200°C/180°C fan-forced.
5 Place tins on oven tray; line pastry with baking paper then fill with dried beans or rice. Bake 10 minutes; remove paper and beans. Bake further 7 minutes or until pastry cases are browned lightly; cool. Reduce oven to 180°C/160°C fan-forced.
6 Meanwhile, make filling.
7 Spoon filling into pastry cases; bake about 25 minutes or until set. Cool.
filling Combine ingredients in medium bowl.

prep + cook time 45 minutes (+ refrigeration) **makes** 4
nutritional count per tartlet 64.7g total fat (26g saturated fat); 4268kJ (1021 cal); 97.5g carbohydrate; 14.6g protein; 4.6g fibre
tip Use pure maple syrup in the nut filling, not maple-flavoured syrup.

shortcrust pastry
(for 23cm flan tin)

1¾ cups (260g) plain flour
150g cold butter, chopped coarsely
1 egg yolk
2 teaspoons lemon juice
⅓ cup (80ml) iced water, approximately

1 Sift flour into bowl; rub in butter.
2 Add egg yolk, juice and enough water to make ingredients just cling together.
3 Knead dough gently on floured surface until smooth. Enclose with plastic wrap; refrigerate 30 minutes.

prep time 10 minutes (+ standing)
nutritional count per quantity 130.9g total fat (83g saturated fat); 8653kJ (2070 cal); 188.6g carbohydrate; 31.7g protein; 10g fibre

variation To make sweet shortcrust pastry sift 1 tablespoon of icing sugar in with the flour.

pastry tips

working with fillo pastry

Work with one sheet of fillo at a time, keeping the rest covered with baking paper, then a damp tea-towel to prevent sheets from drying out. Brush with oil or melted butter, stack another piece on top and repeat. Don't re-freeze fillo as the layers will stick together.

working with ready-made puff pastry

Try to buy commercial pastry made with butter. Use it chilled, and always cut edges with a sharp knife and without dragging pastry so it will rise evenly in delicate layers.

blind baking

A pastry case can be baked blind (empty) to ensure crispness. Line with baking paper and weigh down with dried beans or uncooked rice, then bake as directed and add filling. Beans and rice can be reused for blind baking but not eating.

storing and freezing

All pastry (apart from choux pastry and thawed fillo) can be stored, tightly wrapped in plastic wrap and enclosed in a plastic bag, in the refrigerator for up to a week, or frozen for up to a month. Allow to return to room temperature before rolling or shaping.

bought pastry cases

There are many different types, shapes and sizes of pastry cases available. Some supermarkets stock a small range, but you're more likely to find these cases in specialty food shops and delicatessens.

glossary

almonds

blanched brown skins removed.

flaked paper-thin slices.

ground also known as almond meal.

slivered small pieces cut lengthways.

arrowroot a starch made from the rhizome of a Central American plant, used mostly as a thickening agent.

bacon rashers also called bacon slices.

baking powder a raising agent consisting mainly of two parts cream of tartar to one part bicarbonate of soda.

beetroot also called red beets; firm, round root vegetable.

bicarbonate of soda also called baking soda.

breadcrumbs

fresh bread, usually white, processed into crumbs.

packaged prepared fine-textured but crunchy white breadcrumbs; good for coating foods that are to be fried.

stale crumbs made by grating, blending or processing 1- or 2-day-old bread.

butter we use salted butter unless stated otherwise.

buttermilk originally the term for the slightly sour liquid left after butter was churned from cream, today it is made like yogurt. Sold with milk products in supermarkets. Despite the implication, it is low in fat.

capers grey-green buds of a warm climate shrub, sold dried and salted or pickled in a vinegar brine; tiny young ones (baby capers) are available in brine or dried in salt.

capsicum also called pepper or bell pepper.

caraway seeds the small, half-moon-shaped dried seed from a member of the parsley family; adds a sharp anise flavour when used in both sweet and savoury dishes.

cardamom a spice native to India; can be purchased in pod, seed or ground form. Has a distinctive aromatic, sweetly rich flavour.

cayenne pepper a thin-fleshed, long, extremely hot dried red chilli, usually purchased ground.

cheese

blue mould-treated cheeses mottled with blue veining. Varieties include firm and crumbly stilton types and mild, creamy brie-like cheeses.

cream cheese commonly known as philadelphia or philly; a soft cow-milk cheese with a fat content ranging from 14 per cent to 33 per cent.

fetta Greek in origin; a crumbly textured goat- or sheep-milk cheese having a sharp, salty taste. Ripened and stored in salted whey.

fontina an Italian cow-milk cheese that has a smooth but firm texture and a mild, nutty flavour. It is an ideal melting or grilling cheese. Use mozzarella or taleggio as a substitute.

gruyère a hard-rind Swiss cheese with small holes and a nutty, slightly salty flavour. A popular cheese for soufflés.

mascarpone an Italian fresh cultured-cream product made similarly to yogurt. Whiteish to creamy yellow in colour, with a buttery-rich, luscious texture. Soft, creamy and spreadable, it is used in desserts and as an accompaniment to a dessert of fresh fruit.

parmesan also called parmigiano; a hard, grainy cow-milk cheese originating in the Parma region of Italy. The curd is salted in brine for a month then aged for up to 2 years.

ricotta a soft, sweet, moist, white cow-milk cheese with a low fat content (8.5 per cent) and a slightly grainy texture. Its name roughly translates as "cooked again" and refers to ricotta's manufacture from a whey that is itself a by-product of other cheese making.

chickpeas also called garbanzos, hummus or channa; an irregularly round, sandy-coloured legume. Firm texture even after cooking, a floury mouth-feel and robust nutty flavour; available canned or dried (requires several hours soaking in cold water before use).

chocolate

Choc Bits also known as chocolate chips or chocolate morsels; available in milk, white and dark chocolate. Made of cocoa liquor, cocoa butter, sugar and an emulsifier, these hold their shape in baking and are ideal for decorating.

dark eating also called semi-sweet or luxury chocolate; made of a high percentage of cocoa liquor and cocoa butter, and little added sugar. Unless stated otherwise, we use dark eating chocolate.

milk most popular eating chocolate, mild and very sweet; similar in make-up to dark with the difference being the addition of milk solids.

white eating contains no cocoa solids but derives its sweet flavour from cocoa butter. Very sensitive to heat.

chocolate hazelnut
spread also known as Nutella; made of cocoa powder, hazelnuts, sugar and milk.

cinnamon available in pieces (called sticks or quills) and ground into powder; one of the world's most common spices, it is used as a sweet, fragrant flavouring for sweet and savoury dishes.

cloves dried flower buds of a tropical tree; can be used whole or ground. Has a strong scent and taste; use sparingly.

coconut
desiccated concentrated, dried, unsweetened and finely shredded coconut flesh.

flaked dried flaked coconut flesh.

milk not the liquid inside but the diluted liquid from the second pressing. Available in cans and cartons at most supermarkets.

shredded unsweetened thin strips of dried coconut flesh.

coconut-flavoured
liqueur we use Malibu.

coffee-flavoured
liqueur we use either Kahlua or Tia Maria.

cornflour also known as cornstarch.

corn syrup a sweet syrup made by heating cornstarch with water under pressure. It comes

in light and dark types; used in baking and confectionery. Available in some supermarkets, delicatessens and health food stores.

cream

pouring also called pure cream. It has no additives, and contains a minimum fat content of 35 per cent.

sour thick, commercially-cultured sour cream with a minimum fat content of 35 per cent.

thickened a whipping cream that contains a thickener; a minimum fat content of 35 per cent.

crème fraîche a mature, naturally fermented cream (minimum 35 per cent fat content) having a velvety texture and slightly tangy, nutty flavour. It can boil without curdling.

cumin also called zeera or comino; resembling caraway in size, cumin is the dried seed of a plant related to the parsley family. Has a spicy, curry-like flavour; found as seeds or ground.

custard powder
instant mixture used to make pouring custard; similar to North American instant pudding mixes.

dill also known as dill weed; used fresh or dried, in seed form or ground. Its anise/celery sweetness flavours the food of the Scandinavian countries, and Germany and Greece. Its feathery, frond-like fresh leaves are grassier and more subtle than the dried version or the seeds.

dried cranberries have the same slightly sour, succulent flavour as fresh cranberries. Available in most supermarkets. Also available sweetened.

egg if a recipe calls for raw or barely cooked eggs, exercise caution if there is a salmonella problem in your area.

eggplant also known as aubergine; is actually a fruit and belongs to the same family as the tomato, chilli and potato. Ranges in size from tiny to very large and in colour from pale green to deep purple. Can be purchased char-grilled, packed in oil, in jars.

fennel also called finocchio or anise. A crunchy green vegetable slightly resembling celery; eaten raw in salads, cooked or used as an ingredient.

fish sauce called naam pla (Thai) and nuoc naam (Vietnamese). Made from pulverised salted fermented fish; has a pungent smell and strong taste, use according to taste.

flour

plain also known as all-purpose flour.

rice very fine, almost powdery and gluten-free; ground white rice.

self-raising all-purpose flour with baking powder and salt; make at home in the proportion of 1 cup flour to 2 teaspoons baking powder.

wholemeal also called wholewheat; milled with the wheat germ making it higher in fibre and more nutritional than white flour.

gelatine we use dried (powdered) gelatine, but is also available in sheets called leaf gelatine; a thickening agent made from collagen or certain algae (agar-agar). Three teaspoons of dried gelatine (8g or one sachet) is about the same as four gelatine leaves. The two types are interchangable but leaf gelatine gives a much clearer mixture than dried gelatine; it's perfect in dishes where appearance matters.

ginger

fresh also called green or root ginger; the thick gnarled root of a tropical plant. Store, peeled in a jar of dry sherry and refrigerated, or frozen in an airtight container.

glacé fresh ginger root preserved in sugar syrup; crystallised ginger (sweetened with cane sugar) can be substituted if rinsed with warm water and dried before using.

ground also called powdered ginger; cannot be substituted for fresh.

glacé fruit fruit such as peaches, pineapple and orange cooked in heavy sugar syrup then dried.

golden syrup a by-product of refined sugarcane; pure maple syrup or honey can be substituted.

hazelnuts also called filberts; plump, grape-size, rich, sweet nut with a brown inedible skin. Remove skin by rubbing heated nuts together vigorously in a tea-towel.

ground also called meal; hazelnuts ground to a coarse flour texture.

horseradish cream is a commercially prepared creamy paste consisting of grated horseradish, vinegar, oil and sugar.

kaffir lime leaves also called bai magrood and looks like two glossy dark green leaves joined end to end, forming a rounded hourglass shape. Sold fresh, dried or frozen, the dried leaves are less potent so double the number if using them as a substitute for fresh; a strip of fresh lime peel may be substituted for each kaffir lime leaf.

kumara the polynesian name of an orange-fleshed sweet potato often confused with yam.

lebanese cucumber short, slender and thin-skinned. Probably the most popular variety because of its tender, edible skin, tiny, yielding seeds, and sweet, fresh and flavoursome taste.

lemon grass also known as takrai, serai or serah. A tall, clumping, lemon-smelling and tasting, sharp-edged aromatic tropical grass; the white lower part of the stem is used, finely chopped. Can be found, fresh, dried, powdered and frozen, in supermarkets and Asian food shops.

macadamias native to Australia; fairly large, slightly soft, buttery rich nut. Refrigerate nuts to prevent rancidity due to their high oil content.

maple-flavoured syrup is made from sugar cane and is also known as golden or pancake syrup. It is not a substitute for pure maple syrup.

maple syrup distilled from the sap of sugar maple trees found only in Canada and some states in the USA.

Maple-flavoured syrup is not an adequate substitute.

mayonnaise, whole egg high quality commercial mayonnaise made with whole eggs and labelled as such; some mayonnaises substitute emulsifiers such as food starch, cellulose gel or other thickeners to achieve the same thick and creamy consistency but never achieve the same rich flavour. Must be refrigerated once opened.

milk we use full-cream homogenised milk unless stated otherwise.

sweetened condensed a canned milk product consisting of milk with more than half the water content removed and sugar added to the remaining milk.

mixed spice a classic spice mixture generally containing caraway, allspice, coriander, cumin, nutmeg and ginger.

mushrooms

button small, cultivated white mushrooms with a mild flavour; use when a recipe calls for an unspecified mushroom.

flat large, flat mushrooms with a rich earthy flavour, ideal for filling and barbecuing. They are sometimes misnamed field

mushrooms which are wild mushrooms.

swiss brown also called roman or cremini. Light to dark brown in colour with full-bodied flavour.

mustard

dijon also called french. Pale brown, creamy, distinctively flavoured, mild French mustard.

wholegrain also called seeded. A French-style coarse-grain mustard made from crushed mustard seeds and dijon-style french mustard.

nutmeg a strong and pungent spice ground from the dried nut of an Indonesian evergreen tree. Usually bought ground, the flavour is more intense if freshly ground from the whole nut (buy in spice shops).

oil

cooking spray we use a cholesterol-free spray made from canola oil.

olive made from ripened olives. Extra virgin and virgin are the first and second press, respectively, of the olives and are considered the best; types named "extra light" or "light" refer to taste not fat levels.

peanut pressed from ground peanuts; the most commonly used oil in Asian cooking due to its capacity to handle high heat without burning.

sesame made from roasted, crushed, white sesame seeds; used as a flavouring rather than a cooking medium.

vegetable any number of oils from plant rather than animal fats.

onion

brown and white are interchangeable. Their pungent flesh adds flavour to a vast range of dishes.

green also known as scallion or (incorrectly) shallot; an immature onion picked before the bulb has formed, has a long, bright-green stalk.

red also known as spanish, red spanish or bermuda onion; a sweet-flavoured, large, purple-red onion.

shallots also called french shallots, golden shallots or eschalots; small, elongated, brown-skinned members of the onion family. Grows in tight clusters like garlic.

spring crisp, narrow green-leafed tops and a round sweet white bulb larger than green onions.

orange-flavoured liqueur such as grand marnier and cointreau.

pancetta an Italian unsmoked bacon, pork belly cured in salt and spices then rolled and dried for weeks. Used as an ingredient rather than eaten on its own.

paprika ground dried sweet red capsicum (bell pepper); there are many grades and varieties, including hot, mild, sweet and smoked.

pecans native to the US and now grown locally; pecans are golden brown, buttery and rich. Good in savoury as well as sweet dishes; walnuts are a good substitute.

pine nuts also known as pignoli; not a nut but a small, cream-coloured kernel from pine cones. They are best roasted before use.

pistachios green, delicately flavoured nuts inside hard off-white shells. Available salted or unsalted in their shells; you can also get them shelled.

polenta also cornmeal; a flour-like cereal made of dried corn (maize). Also the name of the dish made from it.

preserved lemon whole or quartered salted lemons preserved in olive oil and lemon juice. Available from delicatessens and specialty food shops. Use the rind only and rinse well under cold water before using.

prosciutto unsmoked Italian ham; salted, air-cured and aged, it is usually eaten uncooked.

quince yellow-skinned fruit with hard texture and astringent, tart taste; eaten cooked or as a preserve. Long, slow cooking makes the flesh a deep rose pink.

rhubarb classified as a vegetable, is eaten as a fruit and therefore considered one. Leaves must be removed before cooking as they can contain traces of poison; the edible crisp, pink-red stalks are cooked.

rocket also known as arugula, rugula and rucola; peppery green leaf eaten raw in salads or used in cooking.

sesame seeds black and white are the most common of this small oval seed. Toast the seeds in a heavy-based frying pan over low heat.

silver beet also called swiss chard or, incorrectly, spinach; has fleshy stalks and large leaves.

spinach also called english spinach and incorrectly, silver beet.

sugar

brown a very soft, fine granulated sugar retaining molasses for colour and flavour.

caster also called superfine or finely granulated table sugar; dissolves easily.

icing pulverised granulated sugar crushed with a little cornflour.

pure icing also known as confectioners' sugar or powdered sugar.

raw natural brown granulated sugar.

tabasco brand-name of an extremely fiery sauce made from vinegar, hot red peppers and salt.

tahini sesame seed paste available from Middle Eastern food stores.

thyme a member of the mint family; the "household" variety, simply called thyme in most shops, is french thyme; it has tiny grey-green leaves that give off a pungent minty, light-lemon aroma. Dried thyme comes in both leaf and powdered form.

tomato

canned whole peeled tomatoes in natural juices; available crushed, chopped or diced, and unsalted or reduced salt. Use undrained.

cherry also known as tiny tim or tom thumb tomatoes; small and round.

egg also called plum or roma, these are smallish, oval-shaped tomatoes much used in Italian cooking or salads.

paste triple-concentrated tomato puree used to flavour soups, stews, sauces and casseroles.

puree canned pureed tomatoes (not tomato paste); substitute with fresh peeled and pureed tomatoes.

semi-dried partially dried tomato pieces in olive oil; softer and juicier than sun-dried, these are not a preserve thus do not keep as long as sun-dried.

sun-dried tomato pieces that have been dried with salt; this dehydrates the tomato and concentrates the flavour. We use sun-dried tomatoes packaged in oil, unless otherwise specified.

turmeric also called kamin; a rhizome related to ginger and galangal. Must be pounded or grated to release its acrid aroma and pungent flavour. Fresh turmeric can be substituted with the more commonly available powder.

vanilla

bean dried, long, thin pod; the minuscule black seeds inside are used to impart a luscious vanilla flavour.

bean paste is made from vanilla pods and contains real seeds. It is highly concentrated and 1 teaspoon replaces a whole vanilla pod without mess or fuss, as you neither have to split or scrape the pod. It can

also be used instead of vanilla extract. It is found in most supermarkets in the baking section.

extract obtained from vanilla beans infused in water; a non-alcoholic version of essence.

vinegar

balsamic originally from Modena, Italy, there are now many on the market. Quality can be determined up to a point by price; use the most expensive sparingly.

cider made from fermented apples.

walnuts as well as being a good source of fibre and healthy oils, nuts contain a range of vitamins, minerals and other beneficial plant components called phytochemicals. Each type of nut has a special make-up and walnuts contain the beneficial omega-3 fatty acids.

worcestershire sauce sauce thin, dark-brown spicy sauce developed by the British when in India; used as a seasoning for meat, gravies and cocktails, and as a condiment.

yogurt we use plain full-cream yogurt unless stated otherwise.

zucchini zucchini also called courgette; small, pale- or dark-green or yellow vegetable of the squash family.

index

393

conversion chart

MEASURES

One Australian metric measuring cup holds approximately 250ml, one Australian metric tablespoon holds 20ml, one Australian metric teaspoon holds 5ml.

The difference between one country's measuring cups and another's is within a two- or three-teaspoon variance, and will not affect your cooking results.North America, New Zealand and the United Kingdom use a 15ml tablespoon.

All cup and spoon measurements are level. The most accurate way of measuring dry ingredients is to weigh them. When measuring liquids, use a clear glass or plastic jug with the metric markings.

We use large eggs with an average weight of 60g.

LIQUID MEASURES

METRIC	IMPERIAL
30ml	1 fluid oz
60ml	2 fluid oz
100ml	3 fluid oz
125ml	4 fluid oz
150ml	5 fluid oz (¼ pint/1 gill)
190ml	6 fluid oz
250ml	8 fluid oz
300ml	10 fluid oz (½ pint)
500ml	16 fluid oz
600ml	20 fluid oz (1 pint)
1000ml (1 litre)	1¾ pints

LENGTH MEASURES

METRIC	IMPERIAL
3mm	⅛in
6mm	¼in
1cm	½in
2cm	¾in
2.5cm	1in
5cm	2in
6cm	2½in
8cm	3in
10cm	4in
13cm	5in
15cm	6in
18cm	7in
20cm	8in
23cm	9in
25cm	10in
28cm	11in
30cm	12in (1ft)

DRY MEASURES

METRIC	IMPERIAL
15g	½oz
30g	1oz
60g	2oz
90g	3oz
125g	4oz (¼lb)
155g	5oz
185g	6oz
220g	7oz
250g	8oz (½lb)
280g	9oz
315g	10oz
345g	11oz
375g	12oz (¾lb)
410g	13oz
440g	14oz
470g	15oz
500g	16oz (1lb)
750g	24oz (1½lb)
1kg	32oz (2lb)

OVEN TEMPERATURES

These oven temperatures are only a guide for conventional ovens.
For fan-forced ovens, check the manufacturer's manual.

	°C (CELSIUS)	°F (FAHRENHEIT)	GAS MARK
Very slow	120	250	½
Slow	150	275 – 300	1 – 2
Moderately slow	160	325	3
Moderate	180	350 – 375	4 – 5
Moderately hot	200	400	6
Hot	220	425 – 450	7 – 8
Very hot	240	475	9

Published in 2010 by ACP Books, Sydney
ACP Books are published by ACP Magazines, a division of PBL Media Pty Limited

ACP BOOKS

General manager Christine Whiston
Editor-in-chief Susan Tomnay
Creative director & designer Hieu Chi Nguyen
Art director Hannah Blackmore
Senior editor Stephanie Kistner
Food director Pamela Clark
Recipe compiler Abby Pfahl
Sales & rights director Brian Cearnes
Marketing manager Bridget Cody
Senior business analyst Rebecca Varela
Operations manager David Scotto
Production manager Victoria Jefferys

Published by ACP Books, a division of ACP Magazines Ltd.
54 Park St, Sydney NSW Australia 2000. GPO Box 4088, Sydney, NSW 2001.
Phone +61 2 9282 8618 Fax +61 2 9267 9438
acpbooks@acpmagazines.com.au www.acpbooks.com.au

Printed by Toppan Printing Co., China.

Australia Distributed by Network Services, GPO Box 4088, Sydney, NSW 2001.
Phone +61 2 9282 8777 Fax +61 2 9264 3278
networkweb@networkservicescompany.com.au
United Kingdom Distributed by Australian Consolidated Press (UK),
10 Scirocco Close, Moulton Park Office Village, Northampton, NN3 6AP.
Phone +44 1604 642 200 Fax +44 1604 642 300
books@acpuk.com www.acpuk.com
New Zealand Distributed by Southern Publishers Group, 21 Newton Road, Auckland.
Phone +64 9 360 0692 Fax +64 9 360 0695 hub@spg.co.nz
South Africa Distributed by PSD Promotions, 30 Diesel Road Isando, Gauteng Johannesburg.
PO Box 1175, Isando 1600, Gauteng Johannesburg.
Phone +27 11 392 6065/6/7 Fax +27 11 392 6079/80 orders@psdprom.co.za
Canada Distributed by Publishers Group Canada
Order Desk & Customer Service 9050 Shaughnessy Street, Vancouver BC V6P 6E5
Phone (800) 663 5714 Fax (800) 565 3770 service@raincoast.com

Title: Pies/food director Pamela Clark
ISBN: 978-1-86396-998-7 (pbk)
Subjects: Cookery (Puddings)
Other authors/contributors: Clark, Pamela
Also titled: Australian women's weekly
Dewey number: 641.8652
© ACP Magazines Ltd 2010
ABN 18 053 273 546
This publication is copyright. No part of it may be reproduced or
transmitted in any form without the written permission of the publishers.

To order books, phone 136 116 (within Australia) or **order online** at www.acpbooks.com.au
Send recipe enquiries to: recipeenquiries@acpmagazines.com.au

Front cover photographer Julie Crespel
Front cover stylist Louise Bickle
Front cover photochef Sarah Wilmot
Additional photography Julie Crespel
Additional styling Louise Bickle
Photochef Sarah Wilmot